Private Policing

Policing and Society Series

Series editors: Les Johnston, Frank Leishman, Tim Newburn

Published titles

Policing, Ethics and Human Rights, by Peter Neyroud and Alan Beckley
Policing: a short history, by Philip Rawlings
Policing: an introduction to concepts and practice, by Alan Wright
Psychology and Policing, by Peter B. Ainsworth
Private Policing, by Mark Button

Private Policing

Mark Button

WILLAN
PUBLISHING

Published by

Willan Publishing
Culmcott House
Mill Street, Uffculme
Cullompton, Devon
EX15 3AT, UK
Tel: +44(0)1884 840337
Fax: +44(0)1884 840251
e-mail: info@willanpublishing.co.uk
website: www.willanpublishing.co.uk

Published simultaneously in the USA and Canada by

Willan Publishing
c/o ISBS, 5824 N.E. Hassalo St,
Portland, Oregon 97213-3644, USA
Tel: +001(0)503 287 3093
Fax: +001(0)503 280 8832
e-mail: info@isbs.com
website: www.isbs.com

First published 2002

ISBN 1-903240-52-2 Paperback
ISBN 1-903240-53-0 Hardback

British Library Cataloguing-in-Publication Data

A catalogue record for this book is available from the British Library

Printed and bound by T.J. International Ltd, Padstow, Cornwall PL28 8RW

Contents

Foreword

Mark Button's study on private policing is particularly timely. The fragmentation of public policing is occurring widely in most common law jurisdictions and this study usefully sets out the history of the public-private relationship in this sphere of activity.

In a speech in 1998, I drew attention to this phenomenon and argued that it was a matter of serious public significance. Freedom from crime and the fear of crime is not a commodity which should be controlled by market forces; on the other hand, the public police do not have and should not claim a monopoly over community safety.

Mark Button carefully traces the development of different types of private policing in the United Kingdom, some of which have little known, surprisingly, significant powers. He also lays out the long history of the effort to regulate the private security industry and, in doing both, makes useful comparisons with developments elsewhere in the western world.

Private policing is here and is here to stay. It has many attractive components but also some unpalatable possibilities. In painting such a comprehensive picture of the whole sector, Mark Button has provided an important and readable guide which will interest both practitioners and students of the subject.

Ian Blair

Deputy Commissioner,
Metropolitan Police Service

Preface

The study of policing has undergone a fundamental shift over the last decade. There has been a growing realisation amongst academics that the police are but one organisation engaged in the process of policing. This change in thinking is largely the result of the recent growth of the private security industry. In fact, in most industrialised countries, the private security industry now generally employs more personnel than the public police. And it is this 'fragmentation' or 'pluralisation' of policing, as some academics have termed it, that has stimulated a growing interest in private security. Less noticeable – although also increasingly subject to research – is the multiplicity of other private, 'hybrid' and voluntary agents engaged in policing. These range from the Royal Society for the Prevention of Cruelty to Animals and trading standards departments of local authorities to the violent vigilante paramilitary organisations of Northern Ireland. These organisations, too, form part of the broad range of bodies and agencies displaying varying degrees of 'privateness' that fall under the broad umbrella of 'private policing'. Despite this growing interest in these types of organisations, there is as yet no up-to-date book that brings together the latest research into this subject area.

The need for a book like this is also illustrated by the growing interest policy-makers have shown in other forms of policing provision. Recent government discussion about the 'extended police family' and about creating stronger partnerships between the public police and other policing agencies demonstrates the need for a deeper understanding of this subject. The issue of patrol, for example, has spawned various new ideas about increasing the uniformed presence on the streets, ranging from accredited private security patrols, to 'hybrid' community and town wardens, to new ranks in the public police. It is essential these decisions are taken based on informed, broad understanding of the nature of private policing.

Reflecting this growth in private provision has been an expansion in higher education and professional bodies of studies related to private security. Although there is a growing body of literature in this area, very few books have sought to place the study of private security within the broader context of 'policing' studies. As such, this book should be a useful tool for the growing numbers of students in this field. There has also been a proliferation of criminology, criminal justice and policing under-graduate and postgraduate courses in recent years. This has resulted in an ever-increasing number of texts and academic journals devoted to these fields. It is hoped this book will supplement this material in its study of the 'extended police family'. This book, therefore, aims to provide a basis for the understanding of private policing, illustrating as it does some of the extensive (but by no means enough) research that is emerging in this area and some of the issues that are likely to be central to the debate over the delivery and effectiveness of policing in the near future.

This book could not have been written without the help of many colleagues and friends. Particular thanks must go to Professor Les Johnston, Barry Loveday, Professor Frank Leishman and Professor Tim Newburn for their comments on earlier drafts of this book, which proved invaluable in its development. The Rt Hon Bruce George MP must also be thanked for the help he has given me in conducting research in this area and in debating the issues explored in the book. Finally I would like to thank Brian Willan for his patience throughout this project.

Mark Button
University of Portsmouth
February 2002

List of tables

List of acronyms

ABI – Association of British Investigators
ACPO – Association of Chief Police Officers
ASIS – American Society for Industrial Security
BEDA – British Entertainment and Discotheque Association
BNFL – British Nuclear Fuels Limited
BS – British Standard
BSIA - British Security Industry Association
BTP – British Transport Police
CAA – Civil Aviation Authority
CCB – Commercial Crime Bureau
CCTV – close circuit television
CIB – Counterfeit Intelligence Bureau
CID – Criminal Investigation Division
CIT – cash-in-transit
CPS – Crown Prosecution Service
DHBP – Dover Harbour Board Police
DTI – Department for Trade and Industry
DWP – Department for Work and Pensions
EHO – environmental health officer(s)
EN – European Norm
Europol – European Criminal Police Office
FACT – Federation Against Copyright Theft
FAST – Federation Against Software Theft
FBI – Federal Bureau of Investigation
FMI – Financial Management Initiative
FSA – Financial Services Authority

GCHQ – Government Communications Head Quarters
HGV – Heavy Goods Vehicle
HMIC – Her Majesty's Inspectorate of Constabulary
HSE – Health and Safety Executive
ICC – International Chamber of Commerce
ICCCCS – International Chamber of Commerce Commercial Crime
    Services
IMB – International Maritime Bureau
IND – Immigration and Nationality Directorate
Interpol – International Criminal Police Organisation
IPI – Institute of Professional Investigators
IPSA – International Professional Security Association
ISI – Inspectorate of the Security Industry
ISO – International Standards Organisation
LAIOG – Local Authority Investigation Officers Group
LGV – Light Goods Vehicle
LOFIT – London Organised Fraud Investigation Team
MCA – Medicines Control Agency
MDP – Ministry of Defence Police
MGS – Ministry of Defence Guard Service
MoD – Ministry of Defence
MOT – Ministry of Transport
MPA – Music Publishers Association
MPGS – Ministry of Defence Provost Guard Service
MPS – Metropolitan Police Service
NACOSS – National Approval Council for Security Systems
NHS – National Health Service
NPM – new public management
NSI – National Security Inspectorate
NSPCC – National Society for the Prevention of Cruelty to Children
NTE – night-time economy
NYPD – New York Police Department
OFGEM – Office of Gas and Electricity Markets
OFTEL – Office of Telecommunications
OFWAT – Office of Water Services
PACE – Police and Criminal Evidence Act
PAYE – Pay As You Earn
PCA – Police Complaints Authority
PF – Police Foundation
PFI – Private Finance Initiative
PIRA – Provisional Irish Republican Army
PMCA – Police and Magistrates Courts Act 1994

PSI – Policy Studies Institute
PSV – Public Service Vehicle
Quango – quasi-autonomous non-governmental organisation
RAF – Royal Air Force
RM – Royal Marines
RSPB – Royal Society for the Protection of Birds
RSPCA – Royal Society for the Prevention of Cruelty to Animals
RUC – Royal Ulster Constabulary
SEU – Social Exclusion Unit
SFO – Serious Fraud Office
SIA – Security Industry Authority
SIB – Special Investigations Branch
SRB – Single Regeneration Budget
SSPCA – Scottish Society for the Prevention of Cruelty to Animals
TSO – trading standards officer(s)
UKAEA – United Kingdom Atomic Energy Authority
UKAEAC – United Kingdom Atomic Energy Authority Constabulary
UKAS – United Kingdom Accreditation Service
URENCO – Uranium Enrichment Company
VAT – Value Added Tax
VFM – value for money
WPP – Wandsworth Parks Police

This book is dedicated to
the late Jane Wilson

Introduction

There has been a considerable increase in the academic study of policing in recent years, which has been reflected in a corresponding growth in academic research, academic courses and publications. This increasing interest in policing, however, has not focused on the process of policing in its entirety. Rather, there has been a preoccupation with the public policing and a lack of concern with the other bodies that are engaged in policing. A cursory glance at the literature on policing, therefore, might lead one to conclude there is only one organisation engaged in policing: the public police. In recent years, however, there has been a growing realisation that, to explore policing fully, one has to investigate a much wider range of agents.

The first study that looked at non-public policing was perhaps that undertaken during the 1980s by Shearing and Stenning, which investigated the increasing significance of the private security industry in Canada (Shearing and Stenning 1981, 1982, 1987a). In the UK, similar studies illustrating the importance of the private security industry were also undertaken around this time (Draper 1978; South 1988). The next stage of research was the recognition there was also a wide range of voluntary, public sector and quasi-public sector organisations engaged in policing (Johnston 1992a; Jones and Newburn 1998). Such has been the change in the focus of the study of policing that, today, much of the literature now considers the 'pluralisation' or 'fragmentation' of policing (Bayley and Shearing 1996; Johnston 2000a). It is recognised, therefore, that policing is undertaken, amongst other bodies, by the public police, other public policing bodies, 'hybrid' policing bodies, and by private security and voluntary organisations. The fashion for what has been termed 'late modern policing' has spawned a growing literature on these different categories of policing agents and organisations.

The realisation that the balance of policing has changed has stimulated a variety of policy initiatives. For example, there has been a growing policy agenda directed at exercising greater control over some forms of policing, particularly private security policing (Home Affairs Committee 1995; Police Foundation/Policy Studies Institute 1996; Home Office 1999). The increasing use of other forms of policing to support and replace the public police has also been considered extensively (Police Foundation/Policy Studies Institute 1996; Policy Action Team 6 2000; Home Office 2001). Finally, identifying the means to bring together different policing organisations into stronger and more efficient partnerships has also been seen as a priority (Police Foundation/Policy Studies Institute 1996; Blair 1998; Home Office 2001).

It is hoped this book will aid in understanding this new policing order by bringing together and analysing the 'plurality' of the organisations and individuals engaged in policing. In doing so it seeks to challenge some of the prevailing assumptions and views on 'late modern policing'. It argues that the 'pluralisation' of policing is much more fragmented than most commentators have previously suggested. It also highlights the large number of organisations – particularly in the public sector – that are engaged in policing roles. In so doing it demonstrates that many of these organisations do have, in fact, long histories, which goes to show that 'fragmentation' is not a new phenomenon as has been suggested and that fragmentation is likely to continue into the future.

Chapter 1 explores what is meant by 'private policing', examines the wide range of organisations engaged in policing and offers new analytical tools to help understand it. To do this, different classifications of policing are assessed to develop a taxonomy that will facilitate the more systematic analysis of policing. Chapter 2 explores the debate about the changing nature of the state, about the 'fragmentation' of policing and about the emergence of a 'risk society'. This chapter places private policing within these theoretical contexts. It then examines the reasons for the recent increase in the size of the private policing industry.

The following chapters survey the different categories of policing identified in the taxonomy of policing. Chapter 3 explores the public police and the ways they have been increasingly subjected to privatisation. The many central and decentralised public policing bodies are investigated in Chapter 4. These organisations have been neglected by researchers, yet many such organisations undertake very important tasks. This chapter also illustrates how even public sector organisations engaged in policing are highly fragmented, and have been for much longer than recent commentators suggest. Chapters 5 and 6 consider the many organisations that fall into this category. Chapter 5 examines some of these organisations that are located at the public end of the spectrum, Chapter 6 those at the private end.

Chapter 7 explores the vast range of individuals and organisations voluntarily involved in policing. This chapter makes use of Johnston's (1992a) distinction between responsible and autonomous citizenship to explore voluntary forms of policing supported by the state and 'vigilante' forms of policing that do not have the backing of the state. Chapter 8 reviews the extensive and growing literature on the private security industry to illustrate the expanding role this industry plays in policing.

Chapter 9 examines patrol in an attempt to explain the 'pluralisation' of policing. It demonstrates how one of the most significant and symbolic functions undertaken by the public police (patrolling the streets) has been hollowed out by private, voluntary and municipal initiatives. It goes on to illustrate the growing range of bodies engaged in patrol and discusses some of the debates over the emergence of what has been termed 'two-tier' and/or 'multi-tier' policing. Chapter 10 evaluates the regulatory structure that governs private security and the limited means by which employees and firms are held to account. It surveys the international experience of private security regulation and compares this with legislation recently introduced into England and Wales. The chapter concludes with a consideration of Loader's (2000) more radical proposals to regulate and to make accountable the broad range of organisations and individuals involved in policing. Chapter 11 contains some concluding remarks about the theoretical, policy and research implications of the emerging policing order.

Chapter 1

What is private policing?

In recent years there has been a growing realisation that research conducted on the subject of policing has not reflected the wide diversity of bodies engaged in this process (Johnston 2000a; Reiner 2000a). Although there has been but limited interest in private policing, research has consistently shown that the private security sector employs more people than the public police in many countries and undertakes a wide range of functions (Cunningham et al 1990; Jones and Newburn 1998; De Waard 1999). Before the various organisations engaged in private policing are considered, however, it is important to identify what is meant by the term 'private policing'. To do this we must examine these terms separately so that we can identify some of the different bodies that fall within the ambit of both 'private' and 'policing'. It is important to stress, however, that an analysis of private policing would justify a book in its own right and that this chapter, therefore, aims at providing only an introduction to this debate, not a definitive answer.

What is policing?

It is important to define what is meant by 'policing' as this term is often misunderstood. Before the middle of the eighteenth century, the term 'policing' encompassed the regulation of government, morals and economy (Johnston 1992a). It was only after this time that the word 'police' began to be associated with the maintenance of order and the prevention of crime. The word 'police', therefore, came to be associated with the body of men that had recently been formed to undertake these functions (ibid.). A problem that has emerged as a consequence of this association that is 'the police' *only* undertake policing. It is important these terms are differentiated, therefore, as many other organisations than 'the police' are engaged in this process. 'The police' refers to a particular organisation while 'policing' refers to a social process of which the former *and other phenomena* are a part (Reiner 1994). It has indeed been recently argued that the vast bulk of policing is carried out by people and organisations other than the police (Rawlings 1995).

The term 'police' is relatively easy to define in comparison to 'policing' (Reiner 1994). The police are the body of men and women employed by the state who patrol the streets, deal with crime, ensure order and who undertake a range of other social service-type functions. Policing, however, is essentially a function of society that contributes to a particular social order that is carried out by a variety of different bodies and agents. Policing must also be distinguished from social control, which consists of virtually everything that contributes to social order. Social control is thus a much more general concept (ibid.). It could include parents, schools, youth clubs, the media and public executions, to name but a few possible agents of social control. It should also be noted there is a long academic debate on what encompasses social control and which it is not possible to discuss in any depth here (see Cohen and Scull 1983). Cohen (1985), however, has criticised the broadness of definition bequeathed upon the concept of social control, suggesting it has turned social control into a 'Mickey Mouse' concept. He has sought to address this amorphousness by restricting the use of this term to the organised ways in which society aims to produce a particular social order. Cohen (ibid.) defines social control as: 'those organised responses to crime, delinquency, and allied forms of deviant and/or socially problematic behavior which are actually conceived of as such'. It is clear, however, that the police and many other bodies are part of the apparatus of social control. This gives a clue as to the essence of policing as it is must be a specific *aspect* of social control.

Reiner (1994) argues that, in essence, policing means those activities aimed at ensuring the *security* of a particular social order and that these activities are designed to achieve these aims. This distinguishes policing from social control in that the latter encompasses all those processes and activities aimed at producing a particular social order. Policing is thus an aspect of social control, encompassing systems of surveillance combined with the threat of sanctions for the breach of a particular order with the ultimate aim of maintaining the security of that particular order. Reiner (ibid.: 722) defines policing as:

an aspect of social control processes which occurs universally in all social situations in which there is at least the potential for conflict, deviance, or disorder. It involves surveillance to discover actual or anticipated breaches, and the threat or mobilization of sanctions to ensure the security of order. The order in question may be based upon consensus, or conflict and oppression, or an ambiguous amalgam of the two, which is usually the case in modern societies.

Thus in the familiar sense the police conduct patrols, undertake investigations, apprehend offenders for breaches of the criminal law and pass on those for whom they have sufficient evidence to the Crown Prosecution Service (CPS) for prosecution. Those found guilty by the courts are then subjected to punishments.

It is clear many bodies are engaged in these processes. Some citizens form vigilante groups to patrol streets and often apprehend offenders to initiate their own 'justice' or hand suspects over to the authorities. Many private security firms patrol areas, conduct investigations and pass on some of the offenders they find to the police. Other public bodies are also engaged in these processes. The Health and Safety Executive (HSE), for instance, undertakes inspections of the workplace, investigates accidents and pursues criminal prosecutions. Policing can also be achieved through technology. Close circuit television (CCTV) is a good example, where the presence of cameras may deter deviant behaviour. Its recordings can also be used for investigating and prosecuting criminals. Speed cameras on roads are another example, where speeding drivers are detected and prosecuted.

Having defined policing, the wide range of bodies engaged in the process can be identified. In a British context, the list might include non-Home Office police forces (Ministry of Defence Police, British Transport Police, etc.); public bodies, such as the HSE, environmental health officers, fraud investigators (local authority and Benefits Agency); charitable bodies, such as the Royal Society for the Prevention of Cruelty to Animals (RSPCA); and the private security industry – to name but a few. Although this chapter goes on to attempt to produce a taxonomy of the wide range of organisations and agents engaged in policing, as this book is largely concerned with 'private' policing, it is important, first, to define what is meant by 'private'.

What is private?

In recent years there has been a growth in the use by some academics of the word 'commercial' rather than 'private' in relation to non-public policing (Johnston 2000a; Loader 2000). 'Commercial' is narrower in definition than private as it excludes voluntary initiatives and in-house security working for public sector organisations. At the same time, however, it includes the public sector's increasingly commercial activities. Therefore to emphasise the public–private dichotomy, the term 'private' presents fewer problems of definition than 'commercial'.

The public–private distinction has been described as one of the 'grand dichotomies' of Western thought (cited in Jones and Newburn 1998: 29). On the face of it, what is public and what is private seems clear cut: public and private are distinguished by the sector to which they belong. If they are part of the government and funded out of taxation, they are public. If they are provided by companies through fees they are private. In between these two extremes, however, there is a 'grey' area that does not fit. This grey area has become more complex in recent years because of privatisation. It therefore becomes necessary to consider the degree of 'publicness' and 'privateness' (ibid.: 30), and numerous criteria can be used to make this distinction.

Benn and Gaus (1983) have identified three dimensions of 'publicness' and 'privateness': access, agency and interest. Access can be further divided into four categories. *Physical access* defines 'publicness' and 'privateness' by the right to be in a place. Locations such as parks and beaches are public when an individual has a right to enter them, whereas locations are private if those controlling them have the power to deny entrance. The second aspect is *access to activities*. Often access to space is linked to activities that are going on there. A meeting that is open to anyone is public. If it is restricted to a specific group, it is private. The third aspect is *access to information*. In some instances information is open to everyone: a university web site providing information on courses is, by definition, 'public'. On the other hand, an intranet providing information to staff only is 'private'. The final aspect relates to *resources*. There are some resources all may have access to, such as a well to drink from. There are, however, resources that only specific individuals may have access to, such as a well only residents of a village may have access to.

The second dimension Benn and Gaus distinguish is agency, which concerns an individual's status. Is the person an agent of the city, community state or nation and thus 'public', or is the individual acting on his or her own account or for a private organisation? In the context of policing, however, this is a grey area as there are some police officers – who are public officials – who work in a private capacity, such as British Transport Police (BTP) officers working for the privatised rail companies. Conversely, there are some privately employed individuals who work for the state, such as prison custody officers in British private prisons.

The final dimension Benn and Gaus identify is the interest served. There has been a long debate on what constitutes the 'public' and 'private' interest. While it would be impossible to do this justice in the space available here, nevertheless in simple terms a body that serves a private interest supports a specific individual, group or organisation only, although this might also coincide with the broader public interest. An individual or organisation that sought to benefit all would serve the public interest.

Jones and Newburn (1998) have identified what they consider to be the most significant factors in conceptualising the public–private dichotomy for policing. These factors are the mode of provision, the source of funding, the nature of the relationship between the provider and user and the employment status of employees. Mode of provision on the public side would include the furnishing of services by the 'state'; the private provision of these services would be through organisations operating in the open market. Source of funding on the public side is through public taxation. On the private side it is through the payment of fees to the providing body. Where the relationship between provider and user is private it is based upon contracts and competition. Where the relationship is public there is often a monopoly of supply, which is frequently provided universally. Finally, private individuals have no special employment status, while many public officials (including constables) hold special powers. It is this final factor that is used later in this chapter to distinguish the degree of 'publicness' and 'privateness' of different categories of policing.

The public–private dichotomy also presents problems because of the complex range of factors that dictate the degree of 'publicness' or 'privateness'. In addressing such problems, Marx (1987) for example, identifies a wide range of questions that should be posed, such as where does the policing occur and who controls and directs the policing? However, Jones and Newburn (1998) identify five sectoral boundaries in which to explore this dichotomy. The first is sectoral: the relationship of the policing body to the state or to the market. The second is the spatial: the 'space' in which particular policing organisations operate. The third is legal: the powers of particular policing personnel. Finally there is a geographical dimension, which reflects the level (local, national or international) in which the policing takes place.

What it is hoped this discussion about the factors that distinguish the public from the private has revealed is that there are a large number of agents and organisations engaged in policing that exhibit characteristics associated with 'privateness'. Indeed, while it is not the purpose of this book to explore the public police in any depth, even these exhibit some of these characteristics and, as a consequence, the increasing influence of the private sector on the public police does warrant consideration. The large number of other central and decentralised public policing organisations also warrant attention because of their neglect in the research and, in some cases, because of their degree of 'privateness'. There are also a number of policing organisations within the state apparatus that exhibit some 'private' characteristics. As already noted, the BTP operates on private space (owned by privatised companies) and is largely funded from these companies. BTP also serves the public interest, and officers of this organisation hold constabulary powers. For these reasons, the full spectrum of these organisations is considered in this book.

Classifying policing

A number of writers have attempted to classify the broad range of agents and bodies engaged in policing. Although Johnston (1992a) does not provide a table of classification as such, he does provide a framework in which to review policing. He identifies four categories of policing: the private security sector, 'hybrid' policing, citizenship and self-policing. By implication there is also the 'public' police.

The private security industry encompasses those firms providing security services and products (which are considered in greater depth in Chapter 8). 'Hybrid' policing embraces all those public bodies (and some private bodies), other than the public police, which are engaged in policing. This includes non-Home Office police forces, local authority trading standards officers (TSO) and Health and Safety investigators, for example. Many of these bodies exhibit varying degrees of 'publicness' and 'privateness'. The full classification of 'hybrid' policing identified by Johnston is outlined in Table 1.1. The third category involves organised and state-sanctioned citizen policing. This includes Neighbourhood Watch and members of voluntary police bodies such as the special constabulary. Finally, self-policing or autonomous citizenship constitutes those activities done by citizens that are beyond the official sanction of the state. These might include vigilante patrols on an estate or the activities of the Provisional Irish Republican Army (PIRA) in 'policing' its own communities in Northern Ireland.

Table 1.1 Johnston's classification of hybrid policing

---

1. *Bodies engaged in functions related to state security.* These include immigration staff, prisons officers, Ministry of Defence Police, Atomic Energy Authority Constabulary and the various military police forces.
2. *Special police forces.* These include police forces created under legislation other than the Police Act 1964, such as British Transport Police, the various parks and docks police forces.
3. *Departments of state.* These include some of the many officials engaged in regulatory, investigative and law enforcement functions employed by government departments. Examples include the Board of the Inland Revenue Investigation Unit, HM Customs and Excise and Department of Social Security Investigators, to name but a few.
4. *Municipal bodies.* These include some of the many local authority staff engaged in regulatory, investigative and law enforcement functions. Examples include environmental health officers (EHOs etc.), TSOs, social workers.
5. *Miscellaneous regulatory and investigative bodies.* This is a catch-all category that covers such bodies as post office investigations and such workers as BBC investigators. It also illustrates the difficulties of classifying these types of bodies.

Source: Johnston (1992a).

Johnston's use of the term 'hybrid' to describe a category of policing has been criticised by Jones and Newburn (1998). In their four-fold classification outlined in Table 1.2, they use the terms 'other bodies of constables' and 'other public policing bodies' to catch those bodies Johnston describes as 'hybrid'. Jones and Newburn (ibid.) argue that Johnston created the 'hybrid' classification in response to the problems of applying the public–private dichotomy. Jones and Newburn's response was to create these two new classifications, which could also be subject to similar criticisms. For example, they could be accused of merely creating two categories in which all public bodies engaged in policing can be placed if they are not private security or the police service. Also, despite rejecting 'hybrid', they use it to describe a new category of space – 'hybrid space' – that falls between the extremes of public and private space. This would seem to suggest that 'hybrid' could be used to describe their two middle categories of policing as well.

In their classification, Jones and Newburn also neglect to acknowledge the significant number of private organisations engaged in policing that are not private security, such as the National Society for the Prevention of

Table 1.2   Jones and Newburn's classification of policing

Home Department police forces
Metropolitan Police Service

Other bodies of constables/special police forces
British Transport Police
Wandsworth Parks Police

Other public policing bodies
Environmental health officers
Benefit fraud investigators

Private security operations
Staffed services (guarding, door supervisors, shopping centres, etc.)
Investigatory services
Installation of security equipment

Source: Jones and Newburn (1998: 122) (adapted to exclude their specific Wandsworth examples).

Cruelty to Children (NSPCC) and the RSPCA. These bodies are clearly engaged in policing but could not be classified as private security. They also fail to note the significant voluntary element in private policing. Nevertheless, their classification provides a basis upon which to construct a taxonomy of policing.

Thus although there are clearly deficiencies with the term 'hybrid', for ease of description 'hybrid' has been used here as a term to describe those public and private bodies that are neither the public police, private security or some form of voluntary initiative. Therefore what is needed is an attempt to break down the wide range of organisations that fall under the 'hybrid' category into further sub-classifications, and a lead in this can be taken from a number of earlier studies.

In 1977, Miller and Luke undertook what was probably the most extensive survey of 'hybrid' policing organisations in the UK. They used a relatively simple system to divide up the different organisations by sector. These sectors are set out in Table 1.3. Some of the organisations included within the scope of their 12 categories no longer exist, and the structure of government has changed significantly since 1977. The abolition of Wages Councils, for example, removed the need for the Wages Inspectorate. New inspectorates and enforcement bodies have also emerged, such as the Environment Agency of England and Wales.

Table 1.3 Miller and Lukes' classification of 'hybrid' policing bodies*

---

1. *Protection of the revenue* (Inland Revenue, Customs and Excise, etc.)
2. *Protection of the currency* (the Treasury's inspectors who police exchange control)
3. *Protection of state expenditure* (Department of Social Security and Ministry of Agriculture, Fisheries and Food)
4. *State security* (Immigration Service, Ministry of Defence Police, etc.),
5. *Protection of the individual from dangerous practices* (environmental health, HSE, etc.)
6. *Enforcing road safety legislation and regulations* (vehicle registration, driving examiners, etc.)
7. *Safety at sea* (mercantile marine superintendents, fishing vessel surveyors, etc.)
8. *Wages and consumer protection* (Wages Inspectorate, trading standards, etc.)
9. *Regulation of commerce* (Companies Investigation Branch, Solicitors Fraud Unit, etc.)
10. *Nationalised industries* (Post Office Investigations Department, electricity, gas, etc.)
11. *Special police forces in transport and associated undertakings* (river and canal police, airport police, etc.)
12. *Special police forces* (Royal Parks Police, Market Police, etc.).

Note:
*Miller and Luke do not use the term 'hybrid' to describe these bodies.
Source: Miller and Luke (1977)

In 1980, Lidstone *et al* drew up a simpler classification. Theirs was a three-fold distinction: the 'civil police' (the 43 constabularies in England and Wales); 'private police'; 'uniformed private security guards'; and 'other statutory forces' (such as the Ministry of Defence Police (MDP)). As Johnston (1992a) illustrates, this classification ignores some of the many other central and local government bodies engaged in policing.

For the purposes of this book, therefore, the 'hybrid' policing sector will be broken down into three further categories: central and de-centralised public policing bodies; specialised police organisations; and non-private security private policing bodies. These are further sub-divided using a variety of categories as listed in Table 1.4. These further categories are more fluid, could have been developed in a number of different ways and are not intended to be mutually exclusive or exhaustive. The division 'hybrid' policing essentially builds upon the two categories Jones and Newburn identified as 'special police forces' and 'other public policing bodies' and provides a new third part to

Table 1.4 Classifying 'hybrid' policing

Central and decentralised public policing bodies
Central policing bodies
Military policing
Protecting the state
Protecting government revenue and expenditure
Protection of the public
Regulatory bodies
Decentralised policing bodies
Specialist policing
Protecting revenue and expenditure
Protection of the public
Regulatory bodies

Specialised police organisations
Ministry of Defence Police
British Transport Police
United Kingdom Atomic Energy Authority Constabulary
Parks police
Special transport police

Non-private Security Private policing bodies
Protecting the public and animals
Protecting the revenue of organisations
Enforcing the decisions of the courts

address their gap and to provide more detail. All public and private policing organisations that are not part of the public police, private security or some form of voluntary initiative fit into this structure.

The first category encompasses the wide range of public policing organisations. These are all located in the public sector. Although they all vary in their degree of 'publicness', some vary to a greater extent than others. This category can be further differentiated into two subgroups: central and decentralised policing bodies.

The second category are specialised police organisations whose officers appear similar to public police officers in appearance, status, standards. etc., but that differ from the public police in a number of ways and which are explored in more detail in Chapter 5. While a case could perhaps be made for including these in the previous category, because of their unique characteristics (some of these constabularies provide services for private companies and also operate in private space) they warrant consideration in their own right. This category encompasses the numerous specialised police organisations whose officers are sworn constables and who hold similar powers to public police officers. They wear uniforms similar to Home Office police officers and are required to meet many of the same standards. They include large organisations (such as the BTP) as well as small bodies (such as the Mersey Tunnels Police). Such police services also exist in other countries. In the USA, for example, many universities have their own police departments which possess similar or comparable powers to ordinary police departments (Kakalik and Wildhorn 1971e).

Finally, in many countries there are again private organisations that are engaged in policing that are not private security companies or in-house security departments. These can be categorised as those organisations that seek to protect the public or animals (such as the RSPCA) and those that seek to protect the revenues of private organisations (such as the Federation Against Copyright Theft (FACT)).

Loader's classification

More recently, Loader (2000) has attempted to build a completely new method of classifying the wide range of organisations engaged in policing. He begins with 'Policing by government', which includes the Home Office constabularies and other national policing bodies, such as the National Crime Squad. Secondly, he identifies 'Policing through government': policing services provided by government but supplied by others, such as the contracting out of certain functions to the private security industry. Thirdly there is 'Policing above government', which encompasses international developments in policing such as Interpol and Europol. Fourthly there is 'Policing beyond government' which refers to the growing market for private policing services as for example when residents on estates purchase their own private patrols. Finally 'Policing below Government', involves both organised surveillance encouraged by the state (such as Neighbourhood Watch) as well vigilantism.

Loader acknowledges that these categories are clearly porous and that significant overlaps may exist. Indeed, private security services could be found in the 'through', 'beyond' and 'below' categories. Further classifications could also be added. 'Policing inside government' involves organisations employed by the government to police its revenue and expenditure, such as the Directorate of Counter Fraud Services. 'Policing above and beyond government' would describe the various international private policing organisations that exist such as the various organisations of the International Chamber of Commerce (which are considered in

Chapter 6). Nevertheless, Loader's classification does represent one of the most innovative attempts to classify policing to date.

Towards a new classification

The central problem in classifying policing has been the 'hybrid' policing issue: the agents and organisations that vary in their degree of 'publicness' and 'privateness' and that are not the public police, private security or some form of voluntary initiative. This grouping could be added to the other categories to create a further classification of policing, as set out in Table 1.5 and drawing upon the best of Johnston's (1992a) and Jones and Newburn's (1998) groupings. The table also illustrates how the degree of 'publicness' and 'privateness' varies between the groupings.

Table 1.5 provides a full classification of the main forms of policing using the four key criteria identified by Jones and Newburn for distinguishing between the public and private sectors. It highlights a spectrum that begins with organisations exhibiting the deepest degree of 'publicness', (public police bodies), and ends with those that demonstrate the greatest degree of 'privateness', (private security). Although based on the UK, it could also be applied to other countries. The public police are

Table 1.5 A classification of policing

Category	Mode	Funding	Relationship	Status
1. Public police bodies (Home Office police forces in the UK)	Pu	Pu	Pu	Pu
2. Hybrid policing bodies: Central and decentralised public policing bodies	Pu	Pu	Varies	Varies
Specialised police organisations	Varies	Varies	Varies	Pu
Private policing (non-private security)	Pr	Pr	Varies	Pr
3. Voluntary policing	Pr	NA	Pu	Pr
4. Private security	Pr	Pr	Pr	Pr

Notes:
1. Pu = public; Pr = private; NA = non-applicable.
2. The above represents a generalisation for each category and there are likely to be particular examples that do not fit into these general categories.

the primary body employed to patrol streets, to maintain order, to deal with crime and to undertake other social service-type functions. They are also usually distinguished through the holding of special powers (in the UK, through the office of constable). In the UK this category encompasses what are commonly known as the 52 'Home Office' police forces. These range from small rural forces (such as the Wiltshire Police) to the Metropolitan Police Service (MPS). In the UK the public policing bodies are decentralised, and this classification could be applied to a national system such as Japan's National Police Agency. Since the focus of this book is 'private policing', these bodies will not be explored in great depth. However, Table 1.5 shows how Jones and Newburn's four categories could be applied to the public police generally. First, the mode of provision is clearly in the public sector as services are delivered by the state and not through the market. Secondly the source of funding is almost totally through local and national taxation. Thirdly, the principle behind the service to offer policing to all who have the right to it, rather than to those who can afford to purchase it. Finally, the officers have the special status of constables. The increasing privatisation of the public police in recent years, however, warrants brief consideration, and Chapter 3 illustrates the specific areas where the public police exhibit degrees of 'privateness'.

The next category encompasses a wide range of public and private organisations under the 'hybrid' grouping. Broadly, three subcategories are identified. 'Central and decentralised public policing bodies' covers the many specialist policing bodies located in the public sector at either a national or local level that undertake specialist policing functions. They usually exhibit most of the characteristics of 'publicness' although, because of the many differences between organisations, it is often difficult to generalise. For instance, in the UK an example that fits this category would be the HSE, which polices health and safety legislation. This body is clearly located in the public sector in terms of mode of provision: it is funded through national taxation, its services are provided to all according to right and officers possess special powers. However, the same category might also include the Directorate of Counter Fraud Services of the NHS. This organisation is clearly located in the public sector and is funded out of taxation for the NHS. However, its officers possess no special status and they provide their services to the NHS only and not the public. It is also worth noting that many large private organisations, particularly insurance companies, have their own in-house counter-fraud departments that undertake similar work. As chapter 4 illustrates, there are many other central and decentralised public bodies that vary in their degree of 'publicness' or 'privateness'. Hence, under this sub-group in Table 1.5 the relationship and status categories are labelled 'varies', rather than public or private.

The second subgroup covers 'Specialised policing organisations'. While many of the police organisations that fit this grouping could be considered a subsection of the previous subcategory, as a result of the privatisation of the many organisations they serve, they have acquired a more ambiguous status. Chapter 5 illustrates that in terms of their mode of provision some of these organisations are located in the private sector (such as the Port of Tilbury Police) whereas others are located in the public domain (such as the Wandsworth Parks Police (WPP)). Some are funded completely by the private sector (such as the Port of Liverpool Police), others a mix (such as the BTP) and some are funded completely by the public sector (such as the Royal Parks Constabulary). In terms of relationship, some (such as the various parks police forces) provide their services free to the public in these parks while others (such as the British Tranport Police) provide their services to the privatised rail companies through special contractual relationships. Finally, all the agents in these organisations are constables who hold the special status and powers associated with this office and who thus exhibit 'public' characteristics.

The final subcategory includes some of the many private organisations engaged in policing who are clearly not part of the private security industry (such as the NSPCC). All these organisations are located in the private sector and receive their funding through private means. The agents employed by these organisations also hold no special status. In terms of relationship, however, some provide their services to the public free of charge (such as the RSPCA) while others provide them to member organisations as part of the fees paid (such the Federation Against Software Theft).

The third main category encompasses the substantial voluntary involvement in policing. This ranges from state-sanctioned special constables to vigilantes and paramilitaries 'policing' their communities in Northern Ireland. They demonstrate private characteristics in terms of mode of provision as they are nearly all located in the private sector. They are also voluntary, so funding – public or private – is not a significant issue. They usually also have no special status and their services are, in most cases, provided to select groups, although there are examples (such as PIRA) who provide their 'services' to whole communities. In terms of relationship, however, they generally provide their services free, usually universally and under no special contractual arrangements – thus illustrating 'public' characteristics.

Fourthly and finally is private security, which is clearly located in the private sector as it provides services through the market, is funded from fees charged to clients, through contractual relationships and whose employees generally do not possess special powers.

Chapter 2

Explaining private policing

A great deal has been written about the changing nature of the state and society in recent years. Using such labels as 'postmodernity', 'late modernity', 'high modernity', 'advanced liberalism', 'post-Keynesianism' and 'risk society', to name just a few (Giddens 1990; Beck 1992, O'Malley and Palmer 1996; Rose 1996, Johnston 2000a). It is not the purpose of this book to become embroiled in such debates, what is common to them all is a consideration of the changing nature of the state and governance and of the changing nature of society. This consideration is important when examining the emergence of private policing because a central tenet of many studies that have sought to explain the growth of private policing is that the character and nature of private policing are inexorably linked to the state, governance and society.

This chapter, therefore, begins by exploring recent discourse about the state, in particular the view that its 'authority' is declining. This leads on to a consideration of the consequent changes in the nature of policing, in particular the emergence of private policing. While the focus of this chapter is on private security, much of the anlysis also applies to other private bodies that are similarly engaged in policing. The reason for this narrow focus is that it is difficult to generalise about these broader, more fragmented bodies who are also engaged in 'private policing'. There is also much less literature to draw upon about the phenomenon of private policing in general. This does serve to illustrate, however, the need for broader theoretical assessments of the wider concept of private policing.

The end of the nation-state?

A great deal has been written in recent years concerning the weakening of the nation-state. Garland (1996) has identified the 'limits of the territorial nation-state', Rhodes (1995) has illustrated 'governing without government', Jessop (1993) the 'hollowing out of the nation-state', Osborne and Gaebler (1992) 'less government, but more governance' and Strange (1996) the 'retreat of the state'. As noted earlier, it is not the purpose of this chapter to examine these views in any depth but, rather, to highlight some of the more salient changes that have been identified.

It is commonly accepted that the sovereignty of the state, its power and its status have increasingly been undermined at an international level. The process of 'globalisation' (an increasing transnational inter-dependence alongside declining geographical and spatial constraints) has led to a decline in the power of the state in some spheres (Johnston 2000a), particularly its power over the economy. The growth of com-munication technologies and the Internet have led to the expansion of a range of activities across borders (including crime) that require greater inter-state co-operation to address them effectively. States have responded to these forces with global alliances and these have, in some areas, also changed the nature of the state. For instance, those countries that are members of the European Union are increasingly subject to regulations passed in Brussels, which they are unable to resist. Countries that are signatories to the European Convention on Human Rights are similarly limited in the legislation they may pass and face fines if they breach the convention. Some states have been forced to accept the decisions of the United Nations, usually backed by the force of the US military (most notably, Iraq has had to abide by UN Security Council decisions on the inspection of its public buildings for evidence it does not have a programme to produce weapons of mass destruction). This trend in cross-border co-operation has not escaped the area of policing (Leishman, *et al* 1996).

The growth of transnational corporations has given rise to private bodies that rival the power of some small states (Strange 1996), and many large transnational corporations similarly rival some industrial states in terms of wealth. Some even ape states by using private armies to secure their corporate goals: a number of corporations, for instance, have used the services of mercenaries to secure mineral reserves in Africa (Shearer 1998).

In many areas of social life, systems have developed that appear to resemble private governments, particularly within some of the larger corporations. In this world of legal pluralism, organisations develop their own rules and enforcement strategies, and apply their own sanctions for those who breach them (Macauley 1986). The dominance of private corporations can sometimes be the equivalent of that of public government over an individual or local community. For instance, many organisations have complex rules and orders, the breach of which may result in fines, reprimands, termination of employment, etc.

Stenning and Shearing (1980) provide a useful illustration here when they describe a major landslide in the mining-company town of Asbestos, Quebec. The mishap resulted in a number of houses being destroyed. The accident was, however, dealt with by the mining company's 'plant protection service' rather than the public police and other public emergency services. This led to one newspaper headline: 'Company "forgot to call" Police Chief.' The importance of such corporations is not new. In the USA, as primary industries began to emerge in rural areas, there was a growth in 'company towns' where the company provided almost all the required services and goods and where state interference was largely absent (Weiss 1978; Couch 1987).

In another, more recent, illustration of the pervasiveness of private security, Shearing and Stenning (1987b) describe the policing of Disney World. They show how Disney controls the behaviour of those who visit, to which is added to the ultimate sanction of removal from Disney World by security staff. Shearing describes how, on a visit to Disney World, his daughter developed a blister and removed her shoe for comfort. Confronted by a security officer dressed as Bahamian police officer, Shearing was asked to put her shoe back on for her 'safety' or face being escorted from the site. Faced with such a choice Shearing, like most parents, complied rather than risk the rage of his children.

The impotence of the modern state to address some of the most basic demands of its citizens has been highlighted at another level. Garland (1996) has argued that the inability of many industrialised countries to address escalating crime rates demonstrates the decline. He argues (ibid.: 448):

> ... the perceived normality of high crime rates, together with the widely acknowledged limitations of criminal justice agencies, have began to erode one of the founding myths of modern societies: namely, the myth that the sovereign state is capable of providing security, law and order, and crime control within its territorial boundaries.

Linked to this Garland also cites the example of 'responsibilisation', where governments have encouraged non-state organisations and individuals to become more involved in policing and crime prevention. This, he argues, marks the retreat of the state towards a more co-ordinating role, rather than a providing role. Such activities include the encouragement of citizens to purchase their own security products, the promotion of Neighbourhood Watch, making use of private and charitable organisations in crime prevention, and making greater use of the private security industry.

Not all commentators, however, have agreed with the 'hollowing out' of the state hypothesis. Herbert (1999), for example, has argued that many of the obituaries of the nation-state in the area of crime control are rather premature. He argues that encouraging of non-state individuals and organisations to become involved in policing and crime prevention is to support the state's activities – for them to become auxiliaries of the state rather than rivals. He also argues that the private security industry may outnumber the public sector in terms of employees but that the roles they generally perform are insignificant and that there are also large overlaps between the public and private sectors in personnel and operations. He suggests that some of the other threats posed to the state (such as the Internet and the growth of international policing) actually provide opportunities for the state to heighten its role but in new forms. Herbert would therefore seem to agree with Mann's (1993: 115) hypothesis that the state is 'diversifying, developing, not dying'. Whatever the debates, almost all commentators agree that the state's role is changing. One consequence of this on policing has been the growth of private provision.

The fragmentation of policing

The state has traditionally been viewed, in terms of Weber's (1948: 78) definition, as: '... a human community that [successfully] claims monopoly of the legitimate use of physical force within a given territory.' In recent years, however, evidence has emerged that questions whether the state still has such a monopoly in policing or even if it ever did. There is a growing body of literature that describes the increasing 'pluralisation' (Bayley and Shearing 1996) or 'fragmentation' (Johnston 2000a) of policing. This refers to the increasing involvement of private (or commercial), municipal and voluntary bodies in policing. This is illustrated by the increase in size of the 'private policing' sector throughout most industrialised countries relative to the public policing sector. In most western countries the numbers employed in the private security industry outnumber those working for the state police (De Waard 1999). Indeed, in the UK research has shown that the private sector could outnumber the public police by as many as two to one (Jones and Newburn 1998; George and Button 2000). As Chapters 4–8 show, there is also a significant body of private, voluntary, 'hybrid' and other public sector organisations and individuals engaged in policing. Many of these organisations have long histories and some of them predate the formation of the modern police. This goes to illustrate that fragmentation, in terms of the broader range of organisations engaged in policing, is not a new phenomenon. What is new in terms of 'fragmentation' is the expansion of private security. The research has also illustrated the comparablity of some of the functions undertaken by the private security industry and the police (Cunningham *et al.* 1990; Jones and Newburn 1998; Button 1999). These and other changes are explored in greater depth later in this book.

Part of the explanation of the fragmentation of policing in many countries lies in government programmes to 'roll back' the state. This has encompassed extensive privatisation programmes where state assets are sold off, public services are contracted out and where public sector organisations have increasingly aped private sector practices. These policies have reduced the size of the 'state apparatus', although this has often meant an extension of the state vis-à-vis the regulation of the private sector. For instance, in the UK the privatisation of public monopolies (such as gas, telecommunications and water) led to the creation of state regulatory bodies such as OFGEM (Office of Gas and Electricity Markets), OFTEL (Office of Telecommunications) and OFWAT (Office of Water Services). Indeed, in the case of the privatisation of prisons and prisoner escorts in England and Wales, state-appointed monitors and controllers have been created to regulate the private operators (Harding 1997; James *et al* 1997).

The concept of the minimum state (even in some of the most right-wing treatises) has always included a provision for the forces of law and order. Hayek (1960), for example, argued for a minimum state, with government restricted solely to the maintenance of law and order. Nozick (1974) similarly argued for a state restricted to a role of protecting against force, theft and fraud and to the enforcement of contracts. It is only the extreme anarcho-capitalists such as Rothbard (1978) who deny any role for the state at all. As Mathews (1989: 1) has written: 'it is widely assumed that whatever may have been implemented in other areas of social life, the provision of laws, punishment and crime control constitute a unique and privileged realm that should be provided by the State.' However, as noted above, the growing pluralisation or fragmentation of policing and criminal justice has challenged the public police's claim to be the primary policing force. These trends have also emerged at a transnational level.

Transnational private policing

Another illustration of the change in modern policing has been the increasing emergence of transnational policing (Sheptycki 1998). Recent years have seen an expansion of police co-operation between different countries and a growing police presence in transnational and supra-national bodies. Organisations such as Europol (the European Criminal Police Office) now transcend traditional forms of co-operation that were based upon the collection, analysis and distribution of information through bodies such as Interpol (the International Criminal Police Organisation) (Walker 2000). Private policing has not escaped (Johnston 2000b): there is now a large global security market containing some very sizeable companies that operate on an international basis (for example, Group 4 Falck, Securitas, Securicor and Wakenhut). Group 4 Falck, for instance, operates in 50 countries has a £1.6 billion turnover, employs 125,000 staff worldwide and provides services from guarding and the management of prisons to the provision of ambulance and fire-fighting services (Group 4 Falck 2001).

Transnational security firms are in some cases exporting their ideas and activities to other countries. For instance, security corporations such as Wakenhut and Corrections Corporation of America (who manage detention facilities in the USA) have exported their ideas and secured business in other countries, most notably Australia and the UK (Shichor 1995). There are also some companies that operate on a global basis in-order to satisfy the demands of their clients, most notably in the area of corporate investigations and risk analysis. For example, a company that fears its products are being counterfeited in another country is likely to receive only limited interest from policing organisations in the UK and perhaps even less in the suspect country. This may lead the firm to a specialist corporate investigator (such as Carratu, Control Risks or Kroll) that has the capability to perform investigations on a global basis. There is similarly a wide range of transnational professional and trade associations (George and Button 2000). One of largest and most influential of these – despite its non-global name – is the American Society for Industrial Security (ASIS), which is a professional body of over 32,000 security professionals based throughout the world. As well as supplying many services and training products, it provides a networking system at an international level. In some fields of security standards are also set at an international level by transnational and supranational organisations (as, for example, for atomic, aviation and maritime security) (Button and George 2001).

Johnston (2000b) argues that transnational private policing has been both under-theorised and under-evaluated. There have, however, been attempts to theorise the emergence of private prisons at the international level, and this theorisation could possibly be applied to private policing. Lilley and Knepper (1992) have argued that an 'international corrections–commercial complex' has emerged that rivals the military industrial complex, and Baldry (1996) has compared the expansion of American private prison operators in Australia to 'neocolonialism'.

Towards a risk society?

A further trend that has been distinguished in the literature and that has had a significant impact on the emergence of private security is society's increasing preoccupation with risk (Giddens 1990; Beck 1992). Individuals and organisations are now obsessed with 'avoiding the worst'. Accounts of this increasing preoccupation with risk have focused on the emergence of a particular style of thinking that emerged in the nineteenth century when sophisticated statistical techniques were employed to manage the aggregate risks associated with health, social and welfare reforms (Johnston 2000a). This shift in thinking led to actuarial and risk-based modes of government. In the twentieth century, with its concern with the control of crime, this trend has manifested itself in the form of crime mapping and offender profiling techniques, amongst other things. These tactics rely on quantitative research, computer software packages and complex calculations to identify the risks and thus to enable an appropriate response to be developed (ibid.).

The same writers have suggested that, across a wide range of areas of social life, individuals and organisations have become more conscious of risk. These concerns include the risks arising from eating certain foodstuffs, to the risk of environmental catastrophe, to the risk of being burgled. A significant concern individuals and organisations have is that associated with crime. People are anxious about the risks to their property as well as to their personal safety; commercial and non-commercial organisations are preoccupied with minimalising losses from fraud, theft, burglary, etc. This concern with crime risks has a direct impact upon the private security industry (for instance increasing anxiety over the risk of being burgled may lead to an individual to purchase an intruder alarm, or a woman's disquiet that she might be raped or assaulted might lead her to purchase of a personal attack alarm to improve feelings of safety).

Many organisations now undertake sophisticated risk-identification and management procedures. The results of these procedures lead to the deployment of particular levels of security: once the risks have been identified and quantified, they need to be managed and reduced. In the case of crime risks, this invariably leads to some form of security service, product or procedure. The British Post Office (now Consignia), for instance, employs a sophisticated risk model for its post offices for robbery, burglary, etc. Information about a post office's location, proximity to motorways, number of previous attacks and certain social indicators are fed into this model and the score that results leads to the application of particular security strategies. Many other organisations have developed similar strategies. And many insurance companies impose security strategies on policy-holders based upon their analysis of risks to individuals or organisations.

This 'risk society' has also led to an increasing demand for security, and this demand may lead to escalating demands for further security. Loader (1997) has argued that private security may actually increase the fear of crime. He argues that the experience of security strategies and products may make individuals more aware of the risks they face. Further, the more protected the areas in which many people work, the more their perception of danger outside these secluded environments. Thus an increasing preoccupation with risk, combined with the impact of the greater use of private security, may contribute towards the demand for more private security.

Explaining private policing

A number of studies have sought to explain the emergence of private policing. These can broadly be divided into 'fiscal constraint' theories and 'structuralist' or 'pluralist' theories (Jones and Newburn 1998). Before looking at these in more detail, certain limitations of these studies must first be addressed. First and foremost is the tendency to explain private policing in terms of its development in the UK and North America. In many (former) communist, third-world and far eastern countries, some of this analysis clearly does not apply. Secondly, in some of the literature there is a tendency to discuss the emergence of 'private policing' when the authors really mean 'private security'. As was noted in Chapter 1, 'private policing' embraces a much wider and more fragmented range of activities than private security and is, therefore, much more difficult to generalise about.

Fiscal constraint theories

Fiscal constraint theories explain the growth of private policing in terms of the inability of the state to meet the demand for services, which has led to the private sector filling the 'fiscal' gap. In the case of policing, demand for the services of the public police has outstripped the resources available and, as a consequence, the private sector has stepped in to fill some of the gaps in provision. Within this approach two distinct schools of thought can be distinguished: the radical and the liberal democratic.

Radical

Radical perspectives view the growth of private policing as an inevitable consequence of the capitalist crisis, where the state draws in the private sector to strengthen its legitimacy (Spitzer and Scull 1977; Weiss 1978; Couch 1987). Much of the writing associated with these views centres on the emergence of industrial capitalism in the USA around the end of the nineteenth century and the beginning of the twentieth century. In many places the coal, iron and steel industries developed in rural areas where state control was not well established. Industrial militancy threatened the corporations of the time, and as a result, companies resorted to private policing. Additionally and as mentioned previously, many of these industrial areas were 'company towns'. The private police forces employed by these corporations went beyond merely keeping the peace and sought to ensure the workers remained obedient while the companies would draw upon their own private forces, they also made use of contractors for investigations and for policing industrial disputes – most famously Pinkerton. As Weiss (1978: 35) has argued: 'The key to its [private detectives] origins rests with an understanding of the need for an obedient working class to power capitalist industrialisation … '

Companies such as Pinkerton provided a range of services that included general property protection services and a range of strike-breaking services, such as labour espionage, strike-breakers, strike-guards and strike missionaries (those who were paid to convince strikers to go back to work) (ibid). The policing practices that emerged, particularly during strikes led to serious confrontations between companies and workers. There were many disputes where the civil rights of striking workers were violated and where some were even killed. Such were the problems throughout this period that 'private police systems' were often subject to congressional reports (see United States Committee on Education and Labor 1971 – a publication of a 1931 report). As the 1931 report argued:

The use of private police systems to infringe upon the civil liberties of workers has a long and often blood-stained history. The methods used by private armed guards have been violent. The purposes have usually been to prevent the exercise of civil rights in the self-organisation of employees into unions or to break strikes either called to enforce collective bargaining or to obtain better working conditions for union members.

These reports considered private security to be private armies/spies, a threat to the public interest, a danger to society and a phenomenon that should be restricted in the roles it should undertake. However, by the time of the Second World War the confrontations between labour and private police forces had declined significantly, although it would be wrong to assume that the 'radical' perspective died with the ending of these large-scale disturbances. Indeed, Spitzer and Scull (1977), in their analysis of the emergence of private policing, identify three periods in its emergence. These are 'policing as piece work', 'private policing in the industrial age' and 'private policing under corporate capitalism'. They argue that under the last, private policing has emerged to deal with the consequences of large-scale enterprises employing substantial workforces. Such consequences include fraud, pilferage, sabotage and investigating the characters of staff, amongst other things. Many of these functions are things the public sector would be unable and unwilling to undertake. Hence private policing has moved from being 'an oppressor' of the labour movement to being an enforcer of corporate order. Indeed, Cohen (1985) has also taken a radical perspective, arguing that the growth of private security is a sinister widening of the net of social control. There is a two-tiered web of social control based upon the public and private sectors, and where the latter could be said to be the more pervasive.

Liberal democratic

The liberal democratic perspective essentially sees the growth of the private security industry as an inevitable consequence of the increasing demands placed on the public police – demands that cannot be satisfied. The private sector has hence stepped in to fill this gap. The first (and most significant) study associated with this growth in private security is Kakalik and Wildhorn's (1971a, 1971b, 1971c, 1971d and 1971e) research as published by the Rand Corporation. This work illustrates the significant role the private security industry plays in preventing crime against corporations. It also emphasises the public police's supportive and complementary role in this area of work, promulgating the idea of the industry being the 'junior partner' in such areas of policing. Until the publication of this research, the private security industry had been seen as either a potential 'private army' or had been dismissed as being unimportant (Shearing 1992). This research, however, turned these ideas on their heads, demonstrating as it did that the private security industry is a positive asset to society that could be developed and utilised more fully. Kakalik and Wildhorn's study was accompanied by a range of further research, published in both the UK and USA, that also demonstrated the growing importance of private policing (Braun and Lee 1971; Scott and MacPherson 1971; Wiles and McClintock 1972; National Advisory Committee on Criminal Justice Standards and Goals 1976; Draper 1978).

In 1976 the US government funded a major study into the private security industry which was undertaken by the National Advisory Committee on Criminal Justice Standards and Goals. This lengthy report amplified the 'junior partner' view set out in Kakalik and Wildhern's work and sought to establish common standards across the private security industry that would improve its effectiveness and efficiency and, therefore, its contribution to policing. The Preface to the report states that: 'The application of the resources, technology, skills, and knowledge of the private security industry presents the best hope available for protecting the citizen who has witnessed the defenses against crime shrink to a level which leaves him virtually unprotected.'

In the mid-1980s yet another US government-funded project was published that took the Rand Corporation ideas contained in Kakalik and Wildhorn's work even further by advocating an 'equal partnership'. The Hallcrest reports (undertaken by Cunningham and Taylor (1985) and Cunningham *et al* (1990)) argued that the private security industry was a 'massively under-utilised resource' and went on to state that it had become the USA's 'primary protective resource'. The reports advocated an increased role for the private sector in crime fighting and crime prevention and called for greater co-operation between the public and private sectors.

There is growing evidence the liberal democratic perspective is beginning to emerge in the UK in both government and police circles. In 1995 (under the last Conservative government) the Home Office set up a Review of Police Core and Ancillary Tasks that, initially, suggested a wide-ranging programme to privatise police roles. Ultimately, however, only relatively minor and uncontroversial policing functions were identified as areas for privatisation. This liberal democratic approach has continued and developed under the New Labour administration. For example, the Crime and Disorder Act 1998 sets out a statutory obligation for the formation of partnerships between the police and other agencies, which may include the private sector agencies. Moreover, in the proposals published in 1999 for the regulation of the private security industry, the government emphasises the important role private security plays in policing and how this role could be improved (Home Office 1999). Such has been the attitude change towards the police that one senior police officer, Ian Blair (former Chief Constable of Surrey Police and now Deputy Commissioner of the MPS), has gone so far as to advocate that private security industry should provide patrols complementary to those of the police. The current government's desire to see a greater uniformed presence on streets (whether the police, municipal forces or private security) has led to the publication of a report that recommends the deployment of a force of 'Neighbourhood Wardens' (Policy Action Team 6 2000).

At the moment the liberal democratic perspective seems to dominate both UK and US thinking about the private security industry The governments of both countries are seeking to expand policing and crime prevention in the face of accelerating crime rates. Private security has thus come to be viewed as a resource that should be developed and improved, with active partnerships being encouraged between the public and private sectors. One of the more worrying aspects of this, however, is a lack of attention to the issues of accountability and civil liberties (Shearing 1993). In the proposals for the regulation of the private security industry in England and Wales, for example, there is no discussion at all about the issue of accountability (Home Office 1999).

Pluralist or structuralist

The pluralist (or structuralist) perspective emphasises the fragmentation of power: it is private corporations and local communities rather than new, state-centred alliances that take on the reins of power. This perspective has links with Focault's (1977) concept of the dispersion of power and of the disciplinary society: with an increasing emphasis being placed on private justice, private government and the settlement of conflict beyond the state, the policing infrastructure is inevitably being widened. Shearing and Stenning (1981) have argued that the growth of private security is linked to the emergence of 'mass private property', where large shopping malls, leisure facilities, workplaces, etc., are policed by private security. In such places there are rules, strategies to enforce these rules and procedures for the resolution of conflict that frequently do not involve the state. While some of these places might be open to the public they are, in reality, private spaces. Such has been the growth of these places, Shearing and Stenning argue, that they constitute the emergence of a 'new feudalism,' where private corporations have the ability to mimic nation-states (see Macauley 1986). Jones and Newburn (1998), however, have questioned the extent to which this concept of 'mass private property' applies to such countries such as the UK, where the large-scale complexes found in North America are much scarcer (albeit growing in number).

Hence, rather than the state becoming involved in new alliances with corporate organisations, there is a fragmentation of power to a multiplicity of micro-networks. Behind these changes lies a significant shift of power from the centre to corporate entities. Many writers have welcomed this decentralisation (so long as power shifts from the centre to local communities rather than corporate entities) but, as Shearing (1993: 228) has argued:

> What the peep through the prism of policing reveals, is the emerging social world is unlikely to be one in which governance is monopolised by states. The hope of many, … is that governance will rest more directly in the hands of the local communities. The fear is that the reality might be pervasive and intrusive corporate governance, in which the interests of capital are more directly pursued than state-centred theories of capitalism ever dreamed could be possible; the state might wither away, but this may not mean a lessening of the hegemony of capital interests.

This perspective also demands more attention is paid to establishing mechanisms of control and accountability for these emerging policing arrangements. There have, however, been few attempts so to do. Loader's (2000) proposals for the establishment of policing commissions, which are discussed in Chapter 10, are the most important example to date.

Chapter 3

The public police privatised

One of the main aims of this book is to demonstrate the wide range of bodies (other than the public police) who are engaged in policing. However, the public police still remain the most important policing organisation in the multiplicity of agencies involved in policing. As the following chapters illustrate, despite the significant policing functions undertaken by some of the organisations engaged in this process, many still rely on the public police to help them perform some of their roles, co-operate with them in a range of areas and recruit many of their staff from the ranks of retired police officers. Given the extensive literature available on the police, it is not necessary to examine the role, structure, and accountability of the public police here (Waddington 1999; Leishman *et al*, 2000; Reiner 2000b). There is one area, however, that does warrant consideration here: how the public police have increasingly been subjected to the policy of privatisation.

In the UK the public police means the 52 constabularies (43 in England and Wales, 8 in Scotland and 1 in Northern Ireland) that can be distinguished from many other policing organisations (including non-Home Office forces), primarily on account of their 'publicness'. That is to say, these police are a public organisation, funded almost totally from public taxation, that provides almost all its services to the public free of charge and that possesses full constabulary powers. Despite this high degree of 'publicness', however, there are areas where increasing degrees of 'privateness' have emerged.

What constitutes privatisation is the subject of much debate. Definitions of privatisation range from a general shrinking of the state to the more precise replacement of public sector workers with private sector workers (Donahue 1989). The underlying theme of all definitions, however, is a reduction in the role of the state and an a priori belief that the private sector is more efficient and effective at providing goods and services (Atkinson 1990). Butler (1991) has identified a range of privatisation policies, starting with the most absolute, the sale of state assets to the private sector. Next comes deregulation, where the regulatory burden on industries is reduced or removed and which may, as a consequence, lead to greater private sector involvement. Thirdly, there is the situation where public authorities contract out to the private sector functions they previously provided themselves. Finally, is the case where the government gives recipients of their services vouchers so they can shop around for the best service. Privatisation must even involve the removal or reduction of subsidies or the provision of tax incentives (Johnston 1991). Where privatisation has not been possible, attempts have been made to introduce private sector practices into the public sector. This has led to the rise of what has become known as the 'new public management' (NPM) or 'managerialism' (Flynn 1997).

It is also important to note that privatisation does not always mean an increasing role for private companies vis-à-vis the state: other 'private' organisations are also involved, such as charities, voluntary organisations, consumer groups, etc. (Johnston 1991).

Privatising the police

A range of different policies has been used in different countries in attempts to privatise the police (Chaiken and Chaiken 1987; Johnston 1992a; Forst and Manning 1999). These range from the complete replacement of police departments with private security staff (O'Leary 1994), to the hiring out of officers to private organisations, to the charging of fees for services provided (Johnston 1992a).

In a major study of how public policing could be provided privately in the USA, Chaiken and Chaiken (1987) identified four mechanisms of privatisation. The first mechanism they called 'default transfer', where the public police are unable (for various reasons) to meet public demand so that the private sector steps in to fill the gap. The second they called 'accommodation and co-operation', where the police informally allow private security personnel to carry out tasks they do not wish to do for themselves, in return for which the public police will provide the private security personnel with additional services. To illustrate this, Chaiken and Chaiken (ibid.) describe how the policing of the homeless in bus and train stations in some locations has been handed over to the security staff.

In return, if the security staff need to deal with a difficult incident at the station, the police will respond immediately. The third type of privatisation they termed 'legislation', where private security personnel have been given specific statute roles and powers. For instance, in some US states retail security staff have been given special powers of arrest and prosecution, which means the public police do not have to become as closely involved. Finally they identified 'contracts', where the government makes specific contracts with the police to carry out certain specified tasks. The main criticism that can be levelled against Chaiken and Chaiken's classification is that it does not embrace all the policies of privatisation that have been applied to the police. For instance, as Johnston's classification (see below) reveals, it does not include the way the public police have embraced more commercial practices, such as sponsorship and charging fees.

Johnston (1991) classifies the privatisation of policing in three ways. First there is direct and indirect 'load shedding'. This is where the police relinquish roles directly to the private sector, or where the private sector usurps the public police because they are unable to provide the service the public want. Secondly, there is 'contracting out', where the government or police contract with a private organisation to undertake a function for which they will remain in ultimate control. Finally, Johnston identifies 'charging fees and selling services', where the public police have increasingly begun to act in a commercial way by charging fees and selling their services. Johnston's classification could be expanded by including within load shedding Chaiken and Chaiken's 'accommodation and co-operation'. Also, by refining Johnston's final category to include 'embracing private sector practices', the broad range of private sector strategies increasingly used by the public police could similarly be included. This chapter uses Johnston's amended classification to evaluate the privatisation of the public police in the UK. International examples, however, will also be used where appropriate.

Load shedding

Under load shedding, funding and services are moved from the public to the private sector. Load shedding can be direct, where the police abandon certain functions, or indirect, where (because of constraints on resources) the police are unable to supply a service and the private sector steps in to fill the gap. A number of functions have already been shed by the public police, and there are yet others where there is significant speculation about their future status. For instance, in 1995, the then Conservative government published a report on 'Police core and ancillary tasks' (the

Posen review – Home Office 1995). This report set out the 'inner core' tasks that should remain the responsibility of police constables; 'outer core' tasks that should be managed by the police but could be undertaken by specials or by civilians or even contracted out; and 'ancillary' tasks, that do not require police management or delivery (ibid.). Initially there were fears, particularly amongst the Police Federation, that the government was aiming for a significant privatisation of police functions. However, the final report made very few radical recommendations and has even been described as a 'damp squib' (Morgan and Newburn 1997: 57).

Over the last 50 years the history of the British police has been one of incremental load shedding. The police no longer check doors are locked and no longer escort cash-in-transit (CIT) vehicles, which they once did routinely (Clayton 1967). Public order policing is also an area where the police have sought to reduce their role. Up to the late 1980s at football matches it was common for numerous police officers to be deployed within the grounds to undertake safety and public-order policing functions. As a consequence of the Hillsborough disaster there were a number of reports into the safety and security strategies employed by the police at football matches, the most important of which was the Taylor report, published in 1990. Following the publication of this report, the football clubs agreed to play a greater role in safety management, with the police concentrating on crime, public order and emergencies. As a consequence, the police presence at most matches has declined significantly and has been replaced by stewards and safety officers. Indeed, some Premiership football matches take place with no police officers in the ground. For example, in 1989 Nottingham Forrest would typically have 150 police officers in the ground supported by 75 stewards. By 1995 this had fallen to (typically) 250 stewards and 22 police officers (Frosdick and Sidney 1997).

Another area where the police have effectively shed their role is the investigation of fraud. During the 1950s and 1960s, if an organisation suffered internal fraud it would be common practice for the police to undertake an investigation. Such is the extent of fraud in many organisations today, however, that the police will require prima facie evidence before they will become involved. They may even expect the organisation concerned to have completed its own investigation first. As a consequence of this (and often for reasons of maintaining control), many organisations have turned to the private sector to undertake the initial and, sometimes, the whole fraud investigation (Gill and Hart 1997a). The police might be pleased not to have to investigate some frauds (which could be a labour-intensive process), but they still pick up the benefits of a successful investigation carried out by the private sector.

A further area of load shedding in recent years has been the response to intruder alarms. Traditionally, the police would respond to any alarm activation. However, with the huge growth in the use of intruder alarms and the consequent increase in false alarms and, hence, drain on police resources, the police have sought to limit their response. In 1995 the Association of Chief Police Officers (ACPO) published a policy on intruder alarms that set out the conditions for a police response. Those intruder alarms that did not meet the conditions or that had been struck off because of repeated failure would no longer receive an automatic response from the police unless there was some additional factor, such as an eye-witness report (Cahalane 2001). This policy and the subsequent 2000 policy have marked a gradual reduction in police response to intruder alarms. Some forces have attempted to go further. The West Midlands Police tried to introduce a policy that would have meant not attending alarm activations on commercial premises between 06.00 and 19.00 hrs on Monday to Saturday unless the call was confirmed. However, after legal action by the British Security Industry Association (BSIA), they were forced to revert to the national policy (BSIA news release, 26 June, 2000). Nevertheless, intruder alarms is an area where the private security industry has stepped in to offer its services and is an area many private security companies would like to see the police shed completely or at least contract out. Another significant police activity that has effectively been usurped by private initiatives is the patrol of public streets (this is the focus of Chapter 9 and so is not discussed here). There has also been a degree of *informal* load shedding in recent years. Many private shopping centres, for example, are now policed by private security officers unless there is a specific demand for a public police presence.

Contracting out

Under this form of privatisation, the public provider retains responsibility for the funding of the service, but contracts it out to the private sector. A wide range of police functions have been contracted out to the private sector, some of which are not directly related to policing, such as catering, cleaning, maintenance, etc. Within the fields of policing and criminal justice, one of the most lucrative examples of contracting out to the private sector has been that of escorting prisoners, following the Criminal Justice Act 1991. Prisoner escorting had previously been carried out by a mix of police and prison officers but, under the new scheme, escorting has been divided into eight areas in England and Wales managed by such companies as Group 4, Securicor and Reliance – in a business worth nearly £100 million per annum and employing almost 3,500 staff (George and Button 2000). The Criminal Justice Act also provided for the contracting out of magistrates court security, and this has also been a considerable growth area for the private sector. In many police forces the security of police premises themselves has also been contracted out (the security of the West Midlands Police headquarters has been contracted out to Burns (Int.) Security Services, for instance). The Metropolitan Police Service (MPS) has also recently embarked upon a project to contract out its 999 emergency service to the private sector (Pengelly 2001). The government's Private Finance Initiative (PFI) has also led to the further contracting out of some policing roles. In Sussex, for example, there is an initiative for the private sector to build, finance and manage custody centres in six sites in the force's area. These centres would be partly staffed by private security personnel.

Linked to contracting out (and arguably the stage before it) is the significant growth in the use of civilians by police forces over the last 20 years. Many of the posts that used to be held by sworn police officers are now held by civilians. For instance, in the West Midlands Police in 1982, there were 1,838 civilians; this had grown to 2,943 by 1992 (Loveday 1993). Some of the functions civilians have taken over include enforcing traffic legislation, dealing with front-desk inquiries, administrative support, scenes-of-crime work, and crime and intelligence analysis, to name just a few of the most significant examples. Indeed, the Wiltshire Constabulary has recently advertised for civilian investigators to undertake minor investigations (Home Office 2001). Hence the civilianisation of police functions is, arguably, just one step from contracting out.

Embracing private sector management practices

Throughout the Conservative governments of the 1980s and 1990s and into the New Labour administration, there has been a gradual application of private sector practices to public sector bodies, and what has been termed 'managerialism' or 'NPM' has been introduced into the public police sector (Leishman, *et al* 1996; Loveday 1999a). Most public sector organisations (including the police) have been subject to the Financial Management Initiative (FMI), that emphasised the three Es – economy, efficiency and effectiveness. The basic principle behind this initiative has been the setting of objectives, the determination of priorities and, ultimately, the encouragement of private sector practices (Morgan and Newburn 1997). The FMI was followed by Home Office circular 114/1983 which encouraged what has become known as 'policing by objectives'.

Since this circular there has been a growing emphasis on value for money (VFM). Indeed, a Home Office circular issued in 1998 obliges constabularies to set annual 2 per cent efficiency gains from the year 1999–2000. This, combined with the introduction of the new public sector procurement regime, 'Best Value', under the Local Government Act 1999, is likely to intensify police managers' preoccupations with the quality and costs of their services (Butler 2000; Waters 2000). The consequence for police managers is likely to be an increased reliance on private sector management practices.

Police reforms have targeted police managers as well as the regime they operate in (Wall 1998; Savage *et al*, 2001). The Police and Magistrates Courts Act (PMCA) 1994 emphasised the 'chief executive' role of the chief constable, who is responsible for managing rather than administering the police service. The PMCA also charged chief constables with the responsibility for managing budgets and introduced performance targets and business interest into police authorities. Another significant develop-ment was the Sheehy inquiry into 'police rewards and responsibilities', whose recommendations were largely rejected (although some, such as performance-related pay for ACPO- ranking officers, were eventually implemented). Some constabularies have appointed accountants to key positions and, in Merseyside, the Chief Constable's team is called the 'Board of Directors' (Loveday 1999a). The recent government plan for the criminal justice system also advocates more secondments to the private sector for senior managers working in the criminal justice system (including the police) (Home Office 2001).

The application of NPM to the public police has been the subject of much research (Morgan and Newburn 1997; Newburn and Jones 1997; Loveday 1999a). However, the focus of this section is the selling of policing services, the charging of fees and the pursuit of sponsorship.

The police have long charged for 'special services', particularly for the officers they provide at football matches and public order events (Gans 2000). Under the Police Act 1964 (now s. 25 of the Police Act 1996):

> The chief officer of police of any police force may provide, at the request of any person, special police services at any premises or in any locality in the police area for which the force is maintained, subject to the payment to the police authority of charges on such scales as may be determined by the authority (cited in Gans 2000: 187).

Under s. 18 of the same Act, the police authority can also supply goods and services to local authorities. It is not the aim here to explore the debate over what constitutes 'special policing services', but, rather, to illustrate some of the services the police have provided. It has been a long-standing practice for the police to charge for the services they provide at football matches and other public events on private land. In recent years, however, some constabularies have offered officers for hire in a much wider range of roles. Liverpool City Council, for instance, has recently 'rented' an additional 12 officers to patrol its city centre at a cost of £350,000 (Liverpool City Council media release, 5 October 2000). Some constabularies have offered their officers to local businesses for special duties, such as South Wales Police, which has hired its officers out to guard factories and business premises (*Cynon Valley Leader*, 1 September 1994). It has also recently been announced that BMW, Mercedes and Lloyds UDT are to fund a complete unit of detectives in the MPS to investigate stolen vehicles (Syal 2001). A *Sunday Times* investigation found Essex police would be willing to supply officers to police a private party for £35.40 per hour (Burke and Byrne 1996). Many other local authorities, health trusts and businesses have also purchased additional police officers.

Such practices occur on a much larger scale in other countries. In the USA, for example, Reiss (1988) found three models of employment of the public police for private purposes. The first was where the officer found secondary employment and charged for his or her services directly. The second was where the unions co-ordinated the officers' secondary employment. In the third, the police department contracted with the organisation for the secondary employment, from which it received a fee to pay the police officer.

The police are also increasingly charging for a range of services they used to provide free of charge. If a car is stolen and the police recover it, some constabularies will charge a fee (usually shared between the police and recovery company). The Vehicle (Crimes) Act 2001 has enabled the police to keep some of the revenues they earn from fines resulting from speed cameras. Thus the police may have a financial incentive to prosecute more offenders.

Through sponsorship, police forces can raise an additional 1 per cent of their budgets. An exposé by *The Sunday Times* illustrated some of the more bizarre sponsorship deals many forces would consider. Posing as executives from a fictional firm called 'Keystone Security' (Keystone Cops!), for the appropriate fee several forces offered to emblazon the firm's name on their vehicles. North Yorkshire police offered to name an anti-burglary campaign after this firm and, in Leicestershire, the police force suggested the name 'Keystone Security' could be posted on the wall of a new police station the force shared with the local authority.

Many forces have received money for advertising commercial companies. Harrods, for instance, has sponsored a police patrol car for the MPS; Thresher sponsored a police van for £10,000; and Avon and Somerset Police have received over £500,000 in sponsorship (Chittenden 2000). Some constabularies have even created companies to market some of their services. For example, Thames Valley Police, in partnership with Surrey Police and Focus Investigative Analysis, established The Innovative Solutions Consortium, which offers a range of training courses to the public and private sectors (Thames Valley Police 2001).

In a similar vein, Bryett (1996) has identified four methods by which privately owned, non-police resources have been given to the public police. At a basic level, monies and physical resources are simply donated to the police. Clearly, however, the donation of large sums of money or resources raises concern over police independence, should an investigation into the donor ever become necessary. At the second level, space is donated. Bryett provides an example from the USA, where the McDonald's food chain gave part of one of its stores as premises for a police station. A third type of private sector aid is the giving of time. This most frequently takes the form of private individuals offering their time as special constables. At another level it might be helping the police in a search for a missing person or for evidence. Finally come joint ventures between the public and private sectors. In Montgomery County in the USA, for example, the local police department worked with IBM to produce a sophisticated computer disaster and security program. In the UK, the PFI has enabled some forces to use the private sector to design, finance, build and manage police facilities. Some of these facilities include police stations and firearms ranges.

The limits to privatisation?

In theory there is no limit to the privatisation of policing as, in theory at least, the state could be completely abolished. In reality, however, in the UK there are political limits to privatisation. As Dance (1990: 294) has argued: 'It is not so simple however, to decide how far privatisation should go. The mere fact that it is possible to dismantle some or all of policing and spread it around other operators is not an argument for doing so: we must consider the implications more closely.' The public police could, nevertheless, be subjected to further privatisation if there was the political will so to do. In this vein, Johnston (1992a) has discussed the hypothetical constabulary of 'Profitshire'. In this model, Johnston considers how a company could be established by the constabulary to sell security services (this has already happened in Northumbria!). One could, however, take the 'Profitshire' model much further.

'Extreme profitshire'

As prisons in the UK have been contracted out in their entirety to the private sector, it could be possible (in theory at least) to contract out of a whole police service or significant functions within it. Given resources issues, it would need to be a small force to begin with. A government might, for example, decide to ask for expressions of interest to provide privatised policing services in Warwickshire after the passage of the hypothetical Police Privatisation Act 2010. This Act sets out a regulatory authority, that awards, monitors and regulates contracts with the private sector. The authority sets out a detailed specification of the standards required and the targets to be met. After a detailed analysis of the tenders, the contract is awarded to a consortium comprising a security company, an employment agency and a merchant bank. This consortium continues to employ the majority of former public sector police officers. These continue to swear the same oath of independence and they possess the same powers. Ultimately, however, their numbers are reduced and they now only undertake what the Posen inquiry described as 'Inner core' functions. 'Outer core' and 'Ancillary' are functions contracted out to private security and investigator firms.

At senior management level, the old managers are replaced by civilians with extensive management experience and with police officers from other forces who have been recruited for their commitment to innovation and reform. The new Chief Constable is the ex-managing director of a very successful and large facilities management company. One of the first decisions the Chief Constable makes is to withdraw from 'inefficient' services, such as responding to intruder alarms and investigating certain property crimes. The Chief Constable also instigates the charging of fees for a range of services that were formerly provided free, such as the investigation of a burglary. More aggressively, the force offers to provide its officers and other staff to businesses at an appropriate rate. The force also pursues sponsorship actively, and all police cars are re-painted a bright orange colour to advertise a major telecommunications company. The officers' uniforms are also emblazoned with a major sponsor, just like professional footballers' shirts.

This is an extreme example (hence the term 'Extreme Profitshire'). However, all the privatisation policies identified have occurred in some form within the UK police service or in comparable sectors, such as prisons. It is therefore not inconceivable that this extreme example could occur if a government was elected with the will to pursue it. The question should therefore be not whether this type of privatisation is possible but, rather, what the implications for policing and for society at large would be if 'Extreme Profitshire' were implemented.

Balancing market forces and public policing

For all the benefits accruing from cost savings and innovation as advocated by the supporters of privatisation (Forst and Manning 1999) there is, however, a wide range of concerns about privatisation. Many of the practices that are emerging or that could be introduced on a large scale could lead to conflicts of interest (Reiss 1988). What if a local business person, for example, who contributed large sums of money to the police through the sponsorship of vehicles is implicated in an investigation into fraud? Could there be a risk the donation might influence the course of the investigation? There is a legitimate concern that commercial interests might corrupt the pursuit of justice. In a similar way, an officer who has been hired out to an organisation may be put under pressure to do what the organisation wants. For instance, a local authority that has hired additional police officers to patrol its town centre (as in the Liverpool example cited above) might use the officers to impose its own order on the area, and this might conflict with some groups' rights. For example, what if there were vagrants sitting on the benches or groups of youths assembled together? This might cause concern amongst shop owners that it lowers the tone of the area and, hence, puts prospective shoppers off. The shop owners might demand these vagrants or youths be removed, despite having committed no crime. The commercialisation of the police might also threaten the generally high regard with which the police are held in the UK (Audit Commission 1996). If they are seen to represent corporate interests who subsequently fall into disrepute, this might have an impact upon them. Simply being associated with certain corporate interests might also have a similar impact.

Perhaps one of the most important concerns about the further privatisation of the police, is the impact the slimmed-down, crime-fighting rump would have. If the public only comes into contact with the police through crime-fighting roles rather than walking the beat, attending public events, etc., this might change the public's perception of the police and of what the police do. There is a genuine fear of divided cities with affluent neighbourhoods policed by client-friendly private security firms and deprived areas policed by an oppressive public police (Davis 1990). There is also the impact such front-line work would have on the remaining police officers – would it damage their health and, therefore, the collective health of the organisation (Dance, 1990)?

Chapter 4

Central and decentralised public policing bodies

In most countries there are two tiers of government: central and local. In some federal jurisdictions such as the USA, however, these governmental divisions are divided even further into central (federal), local (state) and sublocal (cities, counties, etc.) levels of government. Policing organisations often mirror these governmental structures. This chapter, therefore, considers some of the many public bodies in the UK that are engaged in a range of specialised policing and that are situated in either the central or local levels of government. The chapter also illustrates the fragmented nature of this form of policing in the UK, involving as it does dozens of different policing bodies. Finally, while all these policing bodies are clearly located in the public sector, the chapter demonstrates how they vary in their degrees of 'publicness'.

Central policing bodies

There is a multiplicity of central government organisations that are engaged in some form of policing. These organisations are funded from taxation or from other government revenues and they employ personnel who may have special powers but who are not 'sworn' constables. Some of these officers have extensive powers derived from a variety of Acts of Parliament and other regulations. Others have to rely on more subtle and sophisticated means to undertake their duties. Some provide their services to the general public, while others provide them directly to other government agencies or bodies. While there are exceptions to this, most exhibit characteristics associated with the public end of the 'publicness' spectrum. These organisations have been divided here according to their functions. They include military policing organisations, those bodies engaged in the protection of the state, those in the protection of revenue and expenditure, those in the protection of the public and, finally, regulatory bodies.

Military policing

Armed forces personnel are subject to their own military law as well as to civilian law. Breaches of military law are dealt with by the military authorities through courts martial. Some of the more serious offences committed in the UK (such as murder, manslaughter, treason, etc. are dealt with by the criminal courts although, abroad, they may be tried by court martial. Civilians who accompany armed forces personnel abroad may also come under military jurisdiction. Civilians can also be sworn in as special constables in emergency, as they have been on a number of occasions in Northern Ireland. The armed forces policing organisations are divided along service lines into the Corps of the Royal Military Police, the Royal Airforce Police, the Regulating Branch of the Royal Navy and the Royal Marines Police (Miller and Luke 1977). The armed forces themselves have also been used as a policing resource, most notably in Northern Ireland. There has also been some discussion about them undertaking a wider policing role, including acting as special forces targeted at organised crime.

The Corps of the Royal Military Police can trace its origins back to the fourteenth century and comprises a force of 2,000 officers (Defence Committee 1996a) headed by a Provost Marshal. The corps is divided into General Duty Provost Companies who have responsibility for military discipline. These companies deal with incidents involving servicemen and women, with the investigation and reporting of offences reported by servicemen and women, with the recovery of stolen property and with the apprehension of illegal absentees or deserters. The second significant element of the corps is the Special Investigations Branch (SIB), which has responsibility for the investigation of serious, complex or important cases involving servicemen and women. These investigations would include such offences as unnatural deaths, indecency, assaults and drug abuse, to name but a few.

The Royal Air Force Police (RAF Police) is the largest of the service policing bodies with a force of 2,900 (Defence Committee 1996a). It is larger than the other service forces because it also has responsibility for the security of the RAF. When the RAF was originally formed in 1918 it was policed by the Royal Military Police but after a number of ex-Royal

Flying Corps and RAF personnel had received training from the Military Police the RAF Police was formed in 1919 with responsibility for all RAF policing. (RAF Police 1993). The RAF Police is headed by a Director of Security and Provost Marshal. It is organised by region into RAF Provost and Security Services, which undertakes the main, general policing functions. This section also includes specialist investigators and counter-intelligence operations. The other main section is the RAF Police Dogs, which provides patrol, search and demonstration dogs. Some of the activities of the RAF Police include investigating crimes and disciplinary offences, drug and alcohol abuse, flying complaints and the security of the RAF.

The Regulating Branch of the Royal Navy can trace its origins back to 1870, with the formation of the 'Naval Police Branch'. This branch was abolished in 1919, and the Ship's Corporals became Regulating Petty Officers. This reorganisation formed the basis of the modern Regulating Branch. The branch also took on responsibility for both the fleet mail and for detention quarters. The need for officers to patrol the streets onshore to maintain discipline led to the creation of patrol officers, who are now known as Leading Regulators. The Royal Navy Regulating branch has around 443 personnel (Defence Committee 1996a). It has responsibility for discipline, for administrative functions on ships, for naval establishments and for the provision of a service police in naval ports. In Portsmouth there is also the Special Investigations Branch (SIB), which includes a drugs dog detachment. The Royal Navy Regulating Branch is headed by the Provost Marshal and is divided up into the Portsmouth, Plymouth and Scotland regions (as well as the navy training centre and the SIB).

The Royal Marines (RM) Police were formed in 1923 to police HM Dockyards. At the end of the Second World War there were 4,800 RM Police (some 10 per cent of the Royal Marines establishment). In 1948 the Royal Marines Police became the Admiralty Constabulary which later amalgamated with the Army Constabulary to form the Ministry of Defence Police (MDP). In 1964, however, the Royal Marines Police were re-formed to help police the Royal Marines stationed in the Far East. On return to the UK in 1971, it took over garrison policing duties and is now seen as the only 'recognised' policing agency for the Royal Marines, providing all aspects of police duties in such garrison towns as Plymouth, Arbroath, Exeter and Taunton. The Royal Marines Police is headed by an Officer Commanding. Organisationally it has 'uniformed', investigation and training divisions.

The general armed forces have also been used in policing roles. The most obvious example is in Northern Ireland, where the army assists the

Royal Ulster Constabulary (RUC) (now called the Police Service of Northern Ireland) in various policing tasks. As noted earlier, there has been some speculation that the armed forces might become involved in other civilian policing roles. A leaked study by the Defence Research Agency discussed the possibility of the armed forces providing intelligence units to assist MI5 in the bugging of suspected terrorists' homes and in providing special forces to help HM Customs in the covert pursuit of suspects. It also considered the possibility of submarines and warships keeping under surveillance ships and vehicles suspected of carrying contraband or drugs (McManners 1997).

Protecting the state

A number of state bodies are, in a broader sense, engaged in policing. The Security Services (MI5) are probably the most widely known. Along with the Security Intelligence Service (MI6) and GCHC (Government Communications Headquarters Cheltenham), these bodies are engaged in activities to protect national security. MI5 is the most useful body to explore here as the other two are mainly engaged in activities abroad. MI5 is involved, inter-alia, in providing intelligence about threats to the internal security and economic well-being of the UK. It has an annual budget of £120 million and employs 1,860 staff (Norton-Taylor and Black 1998). Its resources are targeted at countering Irish and other domestic terrorism, at international terrorism, espionage, subversion and at the proliferation of nuclear, biological and chemical weapons. The decline of communism and the peace accord in Northern Ireland have led MI5 to seek to expand its role. With the passage of the Security Services Act 1996 it has been successful in this by expanding its role to include 'helping police and customs' to combat serious crime. The accountability of MI5 has long been the subject of public and academic debate and cannot be considered here. There have, however, been repeated concerns over the individual accountability of MI5 agents as well as about the political accountability of MI5. Those interested in this subject are referred to Baxter (1990).

Another significant organisation engaged in state security and policing (in its broadest sense) is the Immigration and Nationality Directorate (IND). The IND, amongst other functions, controls entrance to the UK at airports and ports. IND officers have a considerable range of powers to undertake their duties, mainly under the Immigration Act 1971. These include, inter alia, the right to board a ship or aircraft and to search anything taken off them; the right to examine a person entering the UK; the right to search a person's baggage; the right to examine and retain relevant documents; the right to remove, without warrant, anyone from a ship or aircraft; and the right to detain in custody a person pending a decision to give or refuse entry. Most importantly, however, an immigration officer has the power to arrest without warrant anyone suspected with reasonable cause to have illegally entered the UK, or anyone suspected to have committed or attempted to have breached his or her conditions of entrance.

During the period 1998–99, over 6,000 people were removed from the UK for breach of immigration rules by the IND. There has also been a substantial increase in criminal prosecutions pursued by the IND in recent years. In 1993 only 23 people were prosecuted for facilitating the entry of illegal immigrants. By 1997 this had risen to 139, of which 117 were found guilty (IND 1999). The IND employs around 2,200 personnel who are available for on-entry control, and it has its own body of dogs to help detect clandestine entry by sniffing vehicles and cargoes.

Protecting government revenue and expenditure

Governments generate revenues through a wide range of direct and indirect taxes and, in many cases, also distribute funds to a wide range of individuals and organisations. To prevent and detect fraud in this, central governments have set up governmental departments and quasi-autonomous non-government organisations (QUANGOs) to police these activities. In many cases their operations often lead to prosecutions through the criminal justice system. Table 4.1 identifies some of the main UK government bodies engaged in these functions. The following section briefly explores some of the most important of these bodies, but it should be noted that such is the scope of this subgroup of organisations that their functions often cut across boundaries. For instance, HM Customs and Excise is involved in the protection of revenue through the policing of Value Added Tax (VAT) and duties fraud, but it also has a public protection role in its function of preventing the illegal import of drugs into the UK.

The Inland Revenue is the most important body involved in revenue protection. This government body is engaged in a wide range of activities. Other than policing those who seek to defraud the Inland Revenue, it advises ministers on tax regulations, administers tax law, and assesses and collects tax. To combat tax evasion and fraud, the Inland Revenue employs various specialist investigation teams accounting for around 2,000 staff (Inland Revenue 1999). The Revenue also undertakes general compliance work to identify those working for whom there is no record (ghosts) and to identify those undertaking second jobs but who do not declare this income (moonlighting). Compliance work also involves checking employers' Pay-As-You-Earn (PAYE) schemes and ensuring

Table 4.1. Selected central government policing organisations that protect government revenue and expenditure

Name of organisation	Policing activities
Department of Health – Directorate of Counter Fraud Services	Investigation of fraud and corruption within the NHS and Department of Health
Department for Work and Pensions – Benefits Agency Security Investigation Service	Investigation of fraulent claims for social security
HM Customs and Excise	Investigation of non-compliance in payment of VAT and other duties (amongst other policing roles)
Inland Revenue	Investigation of non-compliance in payment of income and corporation tax (and others)
Ministry of Agriculture, Fisheries and Food Investigation Branch	Investigation of fraud affecting the ministry
Intervention Board Anti-Fraud Unit	Investigation of fraud against Common Agricultural Policy in the UK
Prescription Pricing Authority Fraud Investigation Division	Investigation of fraud by patients and contractors in relation to NHS prescriptions and dispensing

'expenses' are taxed properly. There is also compliance work related to pensions and off-shore funds.

Revenue staff are located in the general tax offices, large business offices and specialist offices. One of the specialist offices is the Special Compliance Office, which undertakes investigations into suspected serious fraud, tax evasion and avoidance, and is the body responsible for instigating criminal proceedings. Revenue staff obtain their powers to pursue their investigations through a complex web of legislation. Many of the offences regarding tax, however, do not reach the criminal courts and are resolved through agreements between the Inland Revenue and the individual/organisation involved or through the 'internal' system of justice. The most serious cases do result in prosecutions by the Inland Revenue. In 1998-99 there were nine prosecutions for false accounts or returns of income, one for false claims to allowances or deductions, seven for false returns for PAYE, six for sub-contractors' exemption fraud, eight for internal fraud, and one for a contrived liquidation (Inland Revenue 1999).

HM Customs and Excise is responsible for bringing in around 40 per cent of central government's total taxation yield (HM Customs and Excise 2001) through VAT and various other excise duties. HM Customs and Excise plays a highly significant role in the policing of fraud concerning these duties, although not all its activities are directly related to this. Its functions also include the administration and collection of customs and excise duties and VAT, advising the Chancellor of the Exchequer on these issues and the compilation of overseas trade statistics. It is, however, its role in the prevention and detection of the evasion of revenue laws and the enforcement of prohibitions and regulations concerning the importation of certain goods that makes it a significant policing body (this brings it into the category of those bodies charged with protecting the public, which are discussed later in this chapter).

HM Customs and Excise has a total of over 25,000 staff. While many of these staff are not directly engaged in investigatory, enforcement and policing functions, one of the most important divisions of HM Customs and Excise is the Investigations Division. This division undertakes amongst other things, work relating to the identification and investigation of drug smuggling; of VAT and other relevant revenue frauds; and identification of fraud involving import/export prohibitions and restrictions. It also collects, analyses, collates and distributes national intelligence relating to customs and excise legislation.

In its role of investigating import/export prohibitions and restrictions, HM Customs has often hit the headlines when it has been involved in major scandals. It was, for instance, involved in the investigation of the 'arms to Iraq' affair, where Matrix Churchill employees were prosecuted for exporting arms to Iraq in contravention of sanctions. The trial subsequently collapsed because of evidence of government support and collusion. More recently, the investigation of the allegedly illegal export of arms to Sierra Leone by the company Sandline International resulted in HM Customs not pursuing a prosecution (Leppard and Rufford 1998). The role its officers play in the criminal justice system is illustrated by the following statistics: during 1996–97, a total of 818 individuals were imprisoned for drugs offences and 18 for other offences as a result of HM Customs investigations (HM Customs and Excise 1997).

The accountability structures of HM Customs and Excise are not as extensive as those of Home Office constabularies. HM Customs is accountable to ministers through Parliament and is also subject to National Audit Office scrutiny. However, despite the fact that HM Customs officers are involved in policing functions and, hence, hold extensive powers, there are no special accountability mechanisms for them. They do not, for instance, fall within the scope of the Police Complaints Authority (PCA). Any complaints against officers would have to be made to the Adjudicator for the Inland Revenue and Customs, the Parliamentary Commissioner for Administration or be made through the courts.

Some of the many benefits given out by the Department for Work and Pensions (DWP) (the government department created in 2001 from the merger of the Department for Social Security and parts of the Department for Education and Employment) are claimed fraudulently. Indeed, in 1994–95 the Benefits Agency (an agency of the DWP until April 2002) recorded 392,000 cases of fraud, which amounted to notional savings of £718 million (Rowlingson *et al* 1997). The 'real' level of fraud, however, is likely to be substantially higher. To combat fraud, the agencies of the DWP employ counter fraud officers. The Benefits Agency investigations division, for example, employs over 3,000 staff. These investigators possess certain limited special powers, such as warrants to obtain certain information and an ability to suspend payments pending further investigations. As with other government bodies, successful investigations usually result in demands for repayment (plus interest). Some of the more persistent and organised fraudsters, however, are prosecuted. In one high-profile case, for example, a fraudster who claimed to be an aristocrat (the Marquis of St Leger), and who was really Keith Alfred Andrews, claimed nearly £20,000 of benefits he was not entitled to while working for Wiltshire County Council. He was found guilty of the fraud and sentenced to 18 months' imprisonment (De Bruxelles 2000).

These investigators also often work with other agencies, including the police. In 1996 Benefits Agency investigators accompanied police on 10,000 roadside vehicle checks for roadworthiness and tachograph offences. Once the police had finished their checks the drivers were handed over to the Benefits Agency investigators, who asked them if they were claiming benefits (MacErlean 1997). In 1998 'Operation Mermaid' involved an even wider range of policing agencies taking part in road blocks, including the police, IND, HM Customs and Excise and the Benefits Agency (Burrell 1998). Conferences have also been held to facilitate multi-agency liaison between the Benefits Agency and other policing bodies. One (held in Scunthorpe and Grimsby in 1998 to discuss fraud), drew over one hundred staff from the Benefits Agency, the police, the Inland Revenue, local authorities, the post office, social services, the IND, Customs and Excise, the Vehicle Inspectorate, the Contributions Agency and the Child Support Agency (cited in Norman and Russell 2000). Following the Grabiner report for the Treasury on the informal economy, there have been calls from the Department of Social Security, the Inland Revenue and HM Customs and Excise to establish a 'special cross-government squad' for a major blitz on fraud (cited in Norman and Russell 2000).

A substantial amount of fraud takes place in the National Health Service (NHS). With a budget of over £40 billion, if fraud amounts to just 1 per cent, this would create a figure of over £400 million! Much of the fraud involves 'patients' claiming free prescriptions they are not entitled to or professionals (such as dentists) claiming fees for work they have not done. To combat this, a National Counter Fraud Service was established in 1998, with 600 staff and a £4 million budget (Laurance 1999). The Prescription Pricing Authority and the Dental Practice Board also have a role to play in the investigation of fraud within the NHS (Norman and Russell 2000).

Protecting the public good

A wide range of central government organisations are engaged in investigative and enforcement functions designed to protect the public good. These generally relate to safety issues (where breaches of the regulations may lead to a risk to safety) or to protecting the public's finances from fraud. These organisations range from the Health and Safety Executive (HSE) whose remit is to enforce and investigate breaches of health and safety legislation, to more specialised bodies such as the Medicines Control Agency (MCA), which enforces and investigates breaches of medicines legislation (see Table 4.2).

The Health and Safety at Work Act 1974 (and various regulations and codes of practice issued under it) created a complex web of standards to ensure safety. The body with responsibility for enforcing this legislation is the HSE, which employs around 1,500 inspectors who possess an impressive range of powers. These include the power to enter premises at any time if there are reasonable grounds for suspecting the premises are dangerous; the power to carry out examinations and investigations within the premises; and the power to seize goods and samples for analysis and evidence. Generally the HSE's approach is non-confrontational, the aim being to improve safety without recourse to sanctions, although inevitably this is necessary on some occasions. In

Table 4.2. Selected central government policing organisations that protect the public good.

Name of organisation	Policing activities
Charity Commission Investigations Division	Investigation of fraud and abuse in charities
Department of Trade and Industry Legal Services Directorate	Investigation of abuse of company legislation and of insider dealing
Environment Agency	Protection of the environment, which includes investigations and prosecutions for breaches of environmental legislation
Financial Services Authority	Supervises banks, regulates investment business and investigates certain financial crime
Health and Safety Executive	Investigation and enforcement of health and safety legislation
HM Customs and Excise	Policing of trade, particularly illicit drugs, firearms and pornography
Marine and Coastguard Agency	Investigation and prosecution of breaches in merchant-shipping legislation
Meat Hygiene Service	Investigation and enforcement of regulations relating to meat industry
Medicines Control Agency	Investigation and enforcement of medicines legislation
Office of Data Protection Commissioner	Investigation and enforcement of data protection legislation
Radiocommunications Agency	Investigation and enforcement of wireless and telegraphy legislation
Serious Fraud Office	Investigation and prosecution of serious fraud

1994–95, for example, the HSE initiated 1,803 prosecutions, of which 1,499 were successful. In the same year the HSE issued 6,512 improvement notices, 124 deferred prohibition notices and 4,172 immediate prohibition notices (Health and Safety Commission 1996). HSE officers often work with the police and other agencies to undertake their work. Prosecutions (if successful) often lead to substantial fines. For example, following the collapse of a tunnel being built at Heathrow airport, Balfour Beaty Civil Engineering Ltd and Geoconsult ZT GmbH were fined over £1.7 million for breaches of health and safety legislation (Health and Safety Executive 2001).

HM Customs and Excise, (which was described earlier) protects the public from illicit drugs, firearms and paedophile material. It also safeguards endangered species. The extent of its activities in this sphere is illustrated by statistics from 1997–98, when officers seized over £3.3 billion worth of drugs, 200 illicit importations of firearms and explosives, and over 3,000 endangered live animals and birds (HM Customs and Excise 2001).

The Radiocommunications Agency is an executive agency of the Department of Trade and Industry with responsibility for the allocation, maintenance and supervision of the UK radio spectrum. One of these responsibilities is the detection and prosecution of unlicensed radio broadcasters. In 1996–97, 851 raids were carried out by investigative staff leading to 51 prosecutions and 51 convictions. In one of these cases the culprit was sentenced to 8 months' imprisonment, although fines and community service are the more common sanction (Radio-communications Agency 2001a). In 2000–2001 there were 84 prosecutions, 84 convictions, over £16,000 of fines imposed and two people were sent to prison for 4 and 6 months respectively (Radiocommunications Agency 2001b).

The Environment Agency has a wide range of functions, including the regulation, improvement and conservation of the environment. In 1999-2000 the agency instigated 4,300 successful prosecutions, leading to the imposition of over £2.8 million worth of fines (Environment Agency 2000). One of the more important policing bodies within the agency are the water bailiffs, who ensure legislation affecting freshwater rivers is enforced and who take measures to deter poaching. These bailiffs hold special powers, mainly conferred under the Salmon and Freshwater Fisheries Act 1984. This legislation also gives them the powers of a constable. It states:

> A water bailiff and a person appointed by the Minister shall be
> deemed for the purpose of enforcement of this Act, or any order or
> bylaw under it, to have all the same liabilities as a constable duly
> appointed has or is subject to by virtue of the common law or of any
> statute (s. 36).

Many examples of the activities of water bailiffs can be found in the press releases issued by the Environment Agency (see Environment Agency 2001). One typical example was the successful prosecution of Kevin Hill for illegally fishing for elvers in March 1998. A night patrol of bailiffs stumbled across Hill unrolling an illegal net into the River Parrett. Hill was convicted and ordered to pay £1,200 costs and to do 180 hours' community service, and he was disqualified from holding any fishing licence for three years (Environment Agency 2001).

The Medicines Control Agency (MCA), which is an executive agency of the Department of Health, has responsibility for ensuring the appropriate standards of safety, quality and efficacy of all medicines on the UK market (Medicines Control Agency 2001). In 1999–2000, over 400 cases of licence infringements were investigated, with a significant number of prosecutions (Medicines Control Agency 2000). The investigators of the MCA are trained to CID (Criminal Investigation Division) standards in interviewing and investigation techniques. Their more familiar investigations range from unlawfully manufactured medicines and counterfeit products to the illegal sale, supply and importation of medicinal products. An example of its work reached the headlines in August 1998, when officers from the agency (along with Westminster Council workers and police officers) raided a Soho bookshop that claimed to be selling the anti-impotency drug Viagra. As Viagra is only available on prescription the bookshop had no right to be selling the drug (Collcutt 1998). Similar to the MCA is the Medical Devices Agency, which undertakes investigations into medical devices, such as wheelchairs and orthopaedic implants, etc., although prosecutions are much rarer in this sphere of medical products.

The Vehicle Inspectorate also pursues activites aimed at protecting the public good. Its responsibilities include heavy goods vehicle (HGV) testing, Public Service Vehicle (PSV) testing, PSV certification and vehicle type approval, administration of the MOT testing scheme, light goods vehicle (LGV) testing, specialised inspections, operator licensing, roadworthiness and traffic enforcement, accidents, defects and recalls. Some of its key policing tasks relate to roadworthiness and traffic enforcement. This involves carrying out roadside and spot checks on vehicles to examine their mechanical condition, tachographs and tax disks. It may also involve checking the authenticity of the HGV and PSV licence holders. Another significant policing activity involves ensuring MOT tests are carried out to the appropriate standard and that there is no fraud. The inspectors have a range of special powers to enable them to undertake their duties. Often, however, they work with the police, particularly on roadside checks. In total around 1,800 staff were employed by the inspectorate in 1992–93, although not all these are directly engaged in policing (Vehicle Inspectorate 1993).

The Serious Fraud Office (SFO) is a specialist government policing body that investigates and prosecutes complex and serious frauds, usually those in excess of £5 million. As fraud ultimately affects the public in some way (the Maxwell pensioners, for instance), the work of the SFO can be considered under this section. In 1997 the SFO had 166 permanent staff, including police officers and chartered accountants. SFO staff often carry out joint investigations with the police, with the Department of Trade and Industry and with the Financial Services Authority (FSA). The SFO, usually, has only a small caseload, which is not surprising given the nature of the fraud it is tasked with investigating. Just over 100 cases were investigated in 1996–97 (Serious Fraud Office 1997). Often, however, these cases are very complex and take a long time to complete.

The Civil Aviation Authority (CAA), amongst many other things, undertakes investigations into the breach of aviation legislation relating to UK aircraft anywhere in the world as well as to foreign aircraft operating in the UK. Another government body dedicated to protecting the public good is the Department of Trade and Industry Investigations and Enforcement Directorate. This directorate has responsibility for investigating commercial malpractice. Its officers have been granted powers, under such legislation as the Companies Act 1985 and the Financial Services Act 1986, to examine company records, amongst other things. Their main areas of investigation relate to insider dealing and the operation of companies. They pursue prosecutions related to insider dealing, insolvencies and disqualified of offenders who have become company directors. The fraudulent activities of those who run charities are investigated by the Charity Commission Investigation Division. Finally, the Financial Services Authority (FSA) has the important task of regulating the financial and services markets. In doing so it undertakes some policing functions to protect consumers by tackling certain financial crime (Financial Services Authority 2001).

Regulatory bodies

Some of the organisations described above are also regulatory bodies in that they seek to set and enforce standards in the private and public sectors. What makes these bodies different from those described in this section is that their activities can lead to criminal prosecutions. There are, however, also numerous other regulatory bodies that never, or extremely rarely, pursue prosections by that, instead, carry out investigations and imposed other forms of punishment. These regulatory bodies can be divided into those that are part of a government department and those that are public but are not part of a government department (usually termed QUANGO). There is no room here to discuss these bodies in full, so Table 4.3 lists a representative selection of just *some* of these bodies, together with their areas of responsibility. Much of the work of these bodies, however, involves some form of policing of 'their' industries or 'professions'. This is largely outside the criminal justice system through their own systems of justice and, sometimes, through the civil courts. Some are involved in the prevention of unregulated activity and will prosecute should this be taking place. Some have dedicated investigatory staff (such as the Gaming Board) while others (such as the general councils) do not.

Table 4.3   Selected National Regulatory Bodies

Regulatory body	Area of responsibility
Gaming Board of Great Britain	Casinos, local lotteries and bingo
General Dental Council	Dentists
General Medical Council	Medical doctors
General Optical Council	Opticians
Independent Television Commission	Independent television
Office of the Rail Regulator	Railways
Office of Electricity Regulation companies	Electricity
Oil and Gas Division of the Department for Trade and Industry	Oil and gas industry
UK Council for Nursing, Midwifery and Health Visiting	Nurses, midwifes and health and health visitors

Decentralised policing bodies

In the UK a significant degree of policing is undertaken at a local level. While it is again difficult to generalise, most exhibit the characteristics associated with 'publicness' (they are located in the public sector, are funded from taxation and other government revenues, provide their services to the public – although in some cases to government bodies – and have officers who often possess special powers.

Specialist policing

Many local authorities employ their own specialist policing bodies. These include Neighbourhood Wardens who provide security and reassurance on problem estates, parks policing bodies (who are 'unsworn'), market policing bodies and forces who police council-owned property. Some local authorities contact private security firms to undertake these functions or have their own in-house security departments. Sometimes, however, there is something more than a private security force, a contract-in firm or in-house organisation. One of the most well known of these in the UK is the Sedgefield Community Force, a local authority body that patrols the public streets (this body is considered in more depth in Chapter 9). Another example is the Birmingham Markets Police, which has around 20 officers. These officers are trained in the requrements of the Police and Criminal Evidence Act 1984 (PACE), first aid, report writing and in dealing with aggression. They police Birmingham markets and enforce local bye-laws. They possess special powers under private legislation and local bye-laws but are not constables. The myriad of private legislation that has allowed for the establishment of these types of forces makes an assessment of their numbers (along with their powers, functions, etc.) extremely difficult. Nevertheless, there are many more market police forces than the Birmingham body. Similarly, many local authorities also have specialist policing bodies for their parks (apart from those discussed in Chapter 6).

At a local level there are also a number of special public authorities that have their own policing personnel. One example is the Broads Authority. This has the status of a National Park Authority and was established under statute. One of its roles is to maintain safe and orderly navigation on the Broads. To achieve this it has a force of 14 river inspectors who enforce the bye-laws, amongst other things. Each year there are around a dozen prosecutions relating to speeding, navigational misdemeanours and toll evasion. British Waterways (who are responsible for canals) also maintain a small patrol staff who carry out similar tasks.

Protecting revenue and expenditure

Local authorities obtain their revenue through local taxes and from this revenue they make payments to a wide range of individuals and organisations. One such payment is housing benefit and, as this benefit is open to fraud, it is the focus of the discussion here (there are, however, local authoriy investigators who deal with other types of fraud, such as council tax evasion).

Housing benefit fraud is estimated to be somewhere in the region of £1 to £2 billion a year (Social Security Committee 1997). A survey by the National Audit Office in 1997 of 65 local authorities found the average number of staff employed to investigate fraud per authority was five. This had increased from a figure of 1.4 in 1992 (National Audit Office 1997). In evidence to the Social Security Committee, the Local Authority Investigation Officers Group (LAIOG) said their investigators came from a wide range of different backgrounds, including auditors, police, benefits staff and employment service staff, as well as from the local authorities themselves. The LAIOG also stated that many investigators were over-worked and were given few resources to carry out their jobs properly. It was also said they lacked some of the powers their colleagues in the Department for Work and Pensions (DWP) possess, such as powers to gain certain information from a suspect. They were also said to be far more limited in their ability to suspend payments pending an investigation (LAIOG 1997).

Jones and Newburn (1998) similarly found that housing benefit investigators in Wandsworth were careful to point out they did not have police powers and that they faced a number of other problems. The most significant of these was the problem of co-ordinating investigations. Many organised frauds cross borough boundaries and may also include other benefits that are the responsibility of the Benefits Agency. Investigations of this type should ideally be pursued in partnership but this is often difficult to achieve. Most investigations result in the local authority seeking the repayment of the monies it has paid out. If there is persistent or organised fraud, however, local authorities will often prosecute and will seek to gain maximum publicity upon conviction. The investigators themselves, however, have often been criticised. An unpublished Audit Commission report leaked to the press detailed how the 'elite' London Organised Fraud Investigation Team (LOFIT) had stopped the benefit of just two claimants since it was set up in 1996 and had brought about only one prosecution. It had been given 98 cases to investigate, of which 12 were fully investigated but resulted in no further action being taken. There were also allegations that new Rovers, Audis and Renaults that were supposed to be used for surveillance work were being used instead for the investigators' own personal benefit (Hencke 1998).

Protecting the public

Local authorities also undertake a wide range of functions related to protecting the public from various hazards and bad practices. Environmental health officers (EHOs) have a wide range of powers related to food hygiene, excessive noise and general public health issues. They possess important powers, such as the right to gain entry to premises, to undertake investigations and even the right to detain in special circumstances. The Public Health (Control of Disease) Act 1984 allows EHOs to remove an unwilling but infectious person to hospital. In certain circumstances EHOs may place various types of orders on individuals and organisations to improve hygiene and, ultimately, they may instigate prosecutions (Jones and Newburn 1998). For example, one major fraud involving 1,300 tons of condemned meat (not fit for human consumption) which was reintroduced to the food chain was jointly investigated by Rotherham EHOs and South Yorkshire police. The five fraudsters (who netted £2.5 million from the fraud) were found guilty and jailed for up to eight years (Stokes 2000).

In a detailed study of EHOs (Hutter 1998), it was found there was generally a culture of persuasion rather than apprehension and punishment. It was also noted in the same study that EHOs were reluctant to be regarded as police officers. Hutter also found that EHOs' decision-making was greatly influenced by their local councils. Councils could affect decision-making through their control of budgets, through the setting of priorities and their decisions as to whom to prosecute. Prosecutions might involve substantial costs, to which a local council might be reluctant to commit resources. It is also not inconceivable that a local councillor could interfere in a particular case or in decisions that could benefit him or her or other interested parties. The question of accountability, therefore, raises issues that require further debate. Indeed to address this, and other issues, Hutter (ibid.) suggested a national body to undertake the functions of EHOs.

A further policing function local authorities undertake relates to trading standards. Training standards officers (TSOs) are charged with various duties from investigating misleading labelling on products and counterfeit goods to searching for checking the accuracy of weights and measures. TSOs possess powers that include the rights of entrance and the rights to seize goods. Like EHOs they may bring about prosecutions although they often employ sanctions that do not make use of the criminal justice system. Jones and Newburn (1998), in their study of Wandsworth, found that officers often required the support of police officers to carry out their duties.

An example of the types of investigation pursued by TSOs is prosecution of the football manager John Burridge, who dressed his team in fake designer clothes. Burridge's prosecution came about after he had been kept under surveillance by the special investigations team of North Yorkshire Trading Standards (*The Independent* 2 July 1998). A further example is the year-long investigation into a Willenhall motor trader who bought cars from auctions and then sold them as if he were a private individual rather than a trader. These activities led to a prison sentence of 18 months (*Walsall Express and Star* 25 May 2000).

Regulatory bodies

Local authorities also regulate the activities of acupuncturists, tatooists, camping sites, dog breeders, knackers' yards, nursing homes, taxis (except hackney carriages in London) and sex shops (Bailey 1992), as well as undertaking investigations into planning proposals. Some of these tasks are undertaken by EHOs while others are done by specialist regulatory staff, such as social services. The regulatory obligations of local authority staff include undertaking inspections, investigating alleged breaches of standards and, sometimes, the pursuit of various types of legal action, including criminal prosecutions.

Chapter 5

Specialised police organisations

In the UK there are organisations engaged in policing that employ staff who hold powers almost identical to those of public police constables (Home Office). These organisations range in size from the Ministry of Defence Police (MDP), which is larger than many Home Office police forces, to the port police forces, which employ only a handful of constables. This chapter, therefore, considers the multiplicity of police organisations that are often referred to as the 'non-Home Office' (or 'Department') police constabularies. These constabularies deserve consideration in their own right because, as a result of privatisation, some of these bodies now operate solely for private companies and organisations and often provide their services to a specific group, company or organisation rather than to the public in general. In a similar way they are not an arm of central or local government, nor are they quangos. This chapter illustrates the varying degrees to which these bodies are characterised by publicness or privateness and it demonstrates how some of these organisations could be regarded as private police forces. The chapter starts with a consideration of the larger organisations (such as the MDP, BTP and UK Atomic Energy Authority Constabulary) before moving on to consider the smaller organisations under the categories of parks police and special transport police.

Ministry of Defence Police (MDP)

The largest of the special constabularies is the MDP, with a strength of around 3,600 officers (Ministry of Defence Police 2000). The MDP can trace its origins back several hundred years to the watchmen who once policed the dockyards. It was the passage of the Special Constables Act 1923, however, which led to the three armed services establishing their own policing forces. These remained separate bodies until 1971, when they were merged to form the MDP. A 1984 House of Commons Defence Committee report, recommended the consolidation of the complex legislation governing the MDP and, in response to this, the Ministry of Defence (MoD) established the Broadbent Committee, whose deliberations culminated in the Ministry of Defence Police Act 1987. This Act extended the jurisdiction of the MDP to 'any place in the UK': first, to Crown, international defence and dockyard property; secondly, for the purposes of securing the unimpeded passage of property; and, thirdly, in respect of visiting forces' personnel and persons subject to the control of, or employed by, the Defence Council or the MoD. Additionally, its jurisdiction was extended to any matter connected with anything done under a contract entered into by the Secretary of State for Defence. MDP officers can also gain additional powers through the enforcement of bye-laws issued under the Military Lands Act 1892. These bye-laws make trespass a criminal offence and authorise constables or Crown servants to remove such trespassers with a view to court action (Johnston 1992b).

The MDP has responsibility for the prevention and detection of crime, for the physical protection of defence establishments and for the security of Crown property. Its most important function, however, is guarding of MoD sites. Like most other police forces, the MDP has both uniformed and detective divisions. It also carries out specialist duties, such as the transport of nuclear materials between Sellafield and the Atomic Weapons Research Establishment at Aldermaston, for which it also provides security. The general rule is that the MDP has responsibility for offences committed by the public or MoD civilians against the MoD, while offences committed by service personnel are the responsibility of the service police (although there are exceptions to this). In garrison towns such as Aldershot, however, the MDP acts like a general police force, dealing with most crimes except the most serious (which are automatically handed over to the local force) (Johnston 1992b).

While the status of the MDP has changed over time, it has increasingly been the subject of debate in recent years. On 1 April 1996, the MDP became a MoD agency under the government's Next Steps Initiative. The aim was to improve the MDP's management to create a more business-like organisation. The initiative also created a unique form of police governance in the UK. The 'owner' of the agency is the second permanent under-secretary of state in the MoD. He (or she) is also chair of the MDP

Police Committee. The MDP Police Committee can set the Chief Constable's budget, can look at disciplinary procedures and can hear reports on operational matters but it cannot give directions to the chief on operational matters. Agency status has also transformed the Chief Constable into the chief executive of the agency. This gave the Chief Constable new freedoms that, it was hoped, would improve the management and efficiency of the force. It remains to be seen how effective these changes will be (Defence Committee 1996a, 1996b).

The Chief Constable's role was a curious one in the past. Until recently it was often filled with senior ex-military personnel with no policing experience although now it is usually filled by a senior officer from a Home Office constabulary. In the MDP tripartite structure, the Chief Constable is responsible for operational matters; the Police Committee is responsible for the maintenance of an efficient force; and the Secretary of State for Defence is answerable for MDP matters in Parliament. The Secretary of State for Defence, however, has much greater power than the Home Secretary vis-à-vis police organisations. The Defence Secretary is ultimately responsible for the MDP and also has the power to hire and fire all MDP officers. In reality, however, it is unlikely that a Chief Constable drawn from a Home Office constabulary of Association of Chief Police Officers (ACPO) rank would tolerate political interference over and above that which occurs in Home Office forces (Johnston 1992b). Another body that ensures the accountability of the MDP is the Police Complaints Authority (PCA), which has jurisdiction over complaints against MDP officers. The MDP is also subject to annual inspections by Her Majesty's Inspectorate of Constabulary (HMIC), although this was only introduced relatively recently.

The MDP has received much political attention, largely in connection with the MoD's attempts to reduce the size of the force in the face of stiff opposition from the House of Commons Defence Committee. Indeed, Johnston (1992b) found a constabulary of over 5,000 officers, compared to 3,600 in 2000. There were three reviews into the force in the 1990s alone. These were *The Defence Police and Guarding Structures Study*, *The Defence Guarding and Manpower Review* and *The MoD Police in the Royal Ordinance Factories – A Consultative Document*. All three reviews advocated the replacement of MDP officers in various areas with either contract security staff, the Ministry of Defence Guard Service (MGS), armed services personnel or guards from the newly created Military Provost Guard Service (MPGS), which comprises armed guard personnel drawn from the services (George and Button 2000).

British Transport Police (BTP)

The BTP are probably the best known of all the non-Home Office police constabularies because of their presence on the railways and on the London Underground. The BTP owe their origins to the various police forces that emerged under private legislation in the nineteenth century to police railway company property. Their roles were to protect the staff and property of the railway companies and to deal with outbursts of public disorder created by navvies during their time off. The BTP itself was created by the British Transport Commission Act 1949. It has declined in numbers from a force of over 5,000 pre-Beeching to just over 2,000 in the year 2000 (British Transport Police 2000). It has also gradually withdrawn from a number of areas of policing, such as canals, waterways, harbours and ports. The most notable change, however, was its replacement by private security officers at Parkeston Quay following the privatisation of Sealink.

Of all the specialised constabularies, the BTP most closely resembles a Home Office constabulary in terms of its structure and functions. It has both uniformed and CID sections with the same rank and promotions structure as Home Office forces. BTP police officers are recruited and trained to Home Office standards, and ACPO-ranked officers sit on various ACPO committees. It also deals with crime that is not significantly different from that dealt with by a Home Office constabulary. It has, however, suffered the most from privatisation.

BTP officers hold constabulary powers 'on, or in the vicinity of trains and premises belonging to or used or leased to users of BTP services and elsewhere to matters relating to those premises' (cited in Jones and Newburn 1998: 125). Thus a BTP officer would have the power of arrest well beyond BTP-policed property for an assault that took place on BTP-policed property. BTP officers have also been given enhanced powers of search in certain areas by the Police and Criminal Evidence Act 1984. There is a degree of ambiguity, however, about their powers. In a very embarrassing lapse of scrutiny under the last Conservative government an oversight when the railways were privatised meant the powers of BTP officers were reduced. This led to legislation being rushed through Parliament in a day, with the Transport Police (Jurisdiction) Act 1994 re-establishing their previous level of powers. When the bill for this Act was passing through Parliament, it was used unsuccessfully by some members to push for an extension of the BTP's constabulary powers to equal those of Home Office constabularies. This was an attempt to address the ambiguity when BTP officers, moving between the locations they police, are often called upon for help by members of the public, who see no difference between them and other constables. During such incidents, BTP officers have to rely upon their citizens' powers and upon the ignorance of the general public. Indeed, during the Bishopsgate bombing, when BTP officers were helping City of London police, one well informed businessman challenged the right of a BTP officer to prevent him returning to his office (Jones and Newburn 1998). BTP officers also fall under the jurisdiction of the Police Complaints Authority (PCA) when it comes to complaints, and are subject to annual inspections from Her Majesty's Inspectorate of Constabulary (HMIC). A BTP committee oversees the force and there are plans to legislate for the establishment of a police authority along the same lines as Home Office police forces.

Concerns have been expressed about the accountability and future of the force following the privatisation of the railways, not least that it might become a 'private police force'. Jones and Newburn (1998) dispute this as it is a condition of the private railway companies' licences that they purchase police services through 'police service agreements' from BTP. They also argue that, although BTP is now largely funded privately, its officers are constables and, as such, have retained operational independence. The question remains, however, as to whether they will retain operational independence when the majority of their funding comes from private companies. There may be further reductions in BTP's size and role as more of the railway companies hire cheaper security officers to provide security on trains. The BTP would no doubt claim they are not replacing BTP officers directly – but might be doing so indirectly. The biggest challenge now facing the BTP is whether it will be able to resist the inevitable calls from the privatised railway companies for more cost-efficient policing and, therefore, for fewer constables and more security officers.

United Kingdom Atomic Energy Authority Constabulary (UKAEAC)

One of the most secretive constabularies in the UK is the UKAEAC, which was formed in 1955 under the Atomic Energy Act 1954. This body provides policing services to the United Kingdom Atomic Energy Authority (UKAEA), British Nuclear Fuels Ltd (BNFL) and Uranium Enrichment Company (URENCO). It had a strength of just over 500 officers in 1999 (UKAEAC 1999), and its main roles include maintaining security at the nuclear installations of the above-named companies, preventing and detecting crime and ensuring the safety of transported nuclear materials (Johnston 1994). Its officers hold constabulary powers on UKAEA (and related) property, within a 15-mile radius of such property and countrywide when escorting nuclear materials. They can also carry firearms without the necessity of a firearms certificate. These powers are set out in the legislation described above and in the Atomic Energy Authority (Special Constables) Act 1976. Officers undergo a 12-week training course and must then pass a two-year probationary period. The UKAEAC (thankfully) deals with very few crimes. The 1999–2000 annual report recorded only 242 offences, of which 173 were theft (UKAEA 2000). Writing in 1992, Johnston found that, since 1977, there had been only 44 arrests on UKAEA property and 9 outside, and that most of these related to theft. However, a single large-scale protest can result in a large number of arrests. For example, during the Easter of 1995, between 250 and 300 Greenpeace protesters cut through fences at Sellafield to protest about the new thermal oxide reprocessing plant – a protest that caused numerous scuffles and over 50 arrests.

When the UKAEAC was originally formed, no structures were in place to create a police authority, just the UKAEA board itself. There is, however, now a police authority comprising representatives from UKAEA, BNFL, URENCO and the Department for Trade and Industry (DTI), plus one independent member elected through agreement between the various bodies, not through legislation. All funds for the UKAEAC are provided by the UKAEA, which gets some of these costs back from other companies that use its policing services. The Chief Constable's budget goes to the finance subcommittee of the police authority, then to the full police authority and, finally, to the board of the UKAEA. This arrangement could affect the force's operational effectiveness as there is significant scope for the UKAEA and the other companies to resist demands for additional expenditure. These pressures have, arguably, been intensified by the privatisation of certain parts of the nuclear industry and through the encouragement of the remaining parts to operate on a commercial basis. It was revealed in April 1998 that the Chief Constable of UKAEAC had resigned over the police authority's refusal to provide the extra police officers he felt were necessary to maintain adequate levels of security (Leake 1998). UKAEAC's officers also come under the jurisdiction of the PCA for complaints made against them. However, the officers' lack of interaction with the general public makes complaints extremely rare. In 1998–99 and 1999–2000, for example, only two and one complaints were received by the PCA (Police Complaints Authority 2000). Questions have been raised, however, about accountability, regarding the UKAEAC's standing orders and the number of inspections carried out by HMIC (Johnston 1994).

It has also been argued that the UKAEAC is nothing more than an expensive security firm (Esler 1983). Its security roles at nuclear facilities are very similar to those of security officers at many other industrial locations – apart from the far more serious consequences should these facilities be attacked successfully. The UKAEAC's low number of arrests and reported crimes also adds weight to this argument. Its limited accountability mechanisms also differentiate it significantly from Home Office police forces. However, replacing the UKAEAC with private security officers (who would probably have to be armed) would make security and policing even less accountable. At the same time, given the standards of the private security industry, such action would raise concerns over security at these sites. One option could be to give the responsibility for security to the military. This could, however, lead the military into conflict with civilians, and it would certainly not address accountability issues or resolve the problem of which force would have primacy should an incident move beyond UKAEA property to the surrounding local constabulary's territory.

One solution that has been suggested is to merge the force with Home Office constabularies, and this action would certainly address concerns over accountability and primacy. However, there remains the question as to whether a Home Office constabulary would be able to bring the same level of expertise to police a nuclear site that one organisation dedicated solely to this task could bring. It would also seem likely that officers would only spend a part of their careers at such sites, and this, too, might lead to a dilution of expertise. Another option would be to merge the force with the MDP, which is probably a more credible option than the former. This would, however, still raise problems of accountability and primacy, and it would also be opposed by the UKAEA and related organisations. The simplest solution would be to reform the constitutional framework that governs the UKAEAC to make it more accountable.

Parks police

Six police organisations have been formed under a range of legislation to police parks. Most of these constabularies (using Jones and Newburn's criteria for distinguishing 'publicness' from 'privateness' outlined in Chapter 1) fall on the public side. They are nearly all located in the public sector (as part of a local authority), they are funded by the local taxpayer, they operate in public space serving the public and they hold constabulary powers. It is their specialist roles, legislative basis and governing structures, however, that distinguish them from the Home Office constabularies.

The largest and best known of these forces is the Royal Parks Constabulary. This body was originally formed in 1872 as the Park Keeping Force, and its officers effectively held the duties and responsibilities of constables within the royal parks. It was not, however, until the passage of the Parks Regulation (Amendment) Act 1974 that park keepers were re-titled 'park constables'. Since its recognition as a police force, it has been subjected to inspection by HMIC. The force has 190 officers and is responsible for policing the royal parks and gardens in Greater London and Hyde Park. It contains ranks from constable up to chief superintendent, and has specialist dog and mounted patrol sections. New recruits undergo much the same training as Home Office police officers, including a 10-week residential course (*Parks Periodical* September 1993). The Royal Parks Police is also the only parks police whose officers fall under the jurisdiction of the PCA (Police Complaints Authority 2000).

The other well-known parks police organisation is the Royal Botanical Gardens Constabulary. This can be traced back to 1844. Other parks constabularies are run by local authorities, such as the Royal Borough of Kensington and Chelsea Parks Police, the Wandsworth Parks Police, Greenwich Parks Constabulary and the Epping Forrest Keepers. The latter are sworn in as constables under the Epping Forrest Act 1878, while the other three are sworn in as constables under s. 18 of the Ministry of Housing and Local Government Provisional Order Confirmation, Greater London Parks and Open Spaces Act 1967. They are all relatively small bodies of 15, 47, 28 and 18 officers respectively (*Police Almanac* 1999).

The Wandsworth Parks Police (WPP) was created in 1985 in response to growing crime rates and disorder in the parks of Wandsworth which the park keepers were unable to deal with. The officers not only police these parks but also leisure centres, cemeteries and libraries, and they effectively act as an in-house security force for the local council. WPP officers undergo a six-week training course and hold constabulary powers in the parks and when enforcing council bye-laws. This has been the subject of contention, but it has been confirmed by legal opinion that the officers do in fact have constabulary powers in the enforcement of bye-laws. There has, however, been one case when an individual who was arrested by the WPP threatened to sue on the grounds of the lawfulness of the arrest. An apology was issued and the officer responsible was reprimanded (Goodwin 1996).

A detailed study of all the arrests made by WPP officers during 1994 found that, of the total of 40 arrests, only 10 per cent related to bye-law offences and that the largest number of arrests (65 per cent) were related to crime (ibid.). It was argued that most of these arrests were based upon the citizen's right of arrest and that, in the majority of cases, they were not lawful (ibid.). The study also illustrated the very small number of arrests made by WPP officers in comparison to MPS officers. This amounted to less than 1 per cent of the arrests made by MPS officers based in Battersea police station, which covers the same area. Unlike Home Office forces the constabulary is not independent, as the Chief Officer is directly accountable to the chair of the Leisure and Amenity Services Committee. Complaints against officers do not fall under the jurisdiction of the PCA. The WPP does, nevertheless, enjoy an excellent working relationship with the MPS. Indeed, one senior officer in Wandsworth told Jones and Newburn (1998) the WPP was an 'invaluable resource'. All prisoners are taken to an MPS station to be charged and held if necessary. Generally, most prisoners are accepted unless there is a question about the legality of the arrest and, sometimes, when there is a new custody officer who is unfamiliar with the WPP. Suspects are fingerprinted and interviewed at MPS stations (ibid.).

Special transport police

The 2000 *Police Almanac* lists 11 different organisations that police such places as ports, tunnels and airports. Some of of these bodies were formed in the nineteenth century. This type of policing organisation, however, has been in decline for some years now, and most were created under a myriad of private legislation, that gave them limited constabulary powers. The ports police have been created in three ways:

1 Through the incorporation of 79–80 of the Harbour, Docks and Piers Clauses Act 1847 into a harbour authority's powers by means of a local Act.
2 Through application to the Secretary of State for Transport for a Harbour Revision Order, made under s. 14 of the Harbours Act 1964.
3 For the Port of London (Tilbury) Authority Police, through incorporation of 79–80 of the 1847 Act (cited above) through local Acts, the most recent of which is the Port of London Act 1968 (Department of Transport 1990).

Of around the 300 ports in the UK it is estimated that approximately 200 could establish a police organisation that possesses constabulary powers.

Table 5.1. Special transport police

Force	Statutory undertaker	Year established	Current legislation	Strength
Port of Tilbury Police	Port of London Authority	1914 (but constables sworn in at West India Dock since 1802)	Port of London Authority Act 1968	25
Belfast Harbour Police	Belfast Harbour Commissioners	—	Belfast Harbour Act 1847*	36
Port of Bristol Police	Bristol City Council	1929	Bristol Dock Act 1848*	45
Port of Dover Police	Dover Harbour Board	1923	Dover Harbour Act 1923*	51
Falmouth Docks Police	Falmouth Dock and Engineering Co.	1845	Falmouth Dock Act 1859*	8
Port of Felixstowe Police	Felixstowe Dock and Railway Co.	1975	Felixstowe Dock and Railway Act 1968*	34
Larne Harbour Police	Larne Harbour Ltd	—	Larne Harbour Act 1847*	16

Port of Liverpool Police	Mersey Docks and Harbour Co.	1811 (earliest known force, current 1975)	Mersey Docks and Harbour (Police) Order 1975**	72
Mersey Tunnels Polce	Merseyside Passenger Transport Authority	1936	County of Merseyside Act 1980 as amended by Local Government Act 1985	82
Belfast International Airport Constabulary	Belfast International Airport	—	Current Airport (Northern Ireland) Order 1994	—
Tees and Hartlepool Police	Tees and Hartlepool Port Authority Ltd	1904	Tees and Hartlepool Authority Act 1966	21

Notes:
*Incorporates s. 79 of the Harbour Docks and Piers Clauses Act 1847.
**Made under s. 14 of the Harbours Act 1964.
Source: Department of Transport (1990), Mersey Tunnels Police promotional literature and Police Constabulary *Almanac* (1998 and 2000).
NB: It was not possible to secure all the information for all these organisations.

In 1990 the Department of Transport found that in fact only 12 had. The Belfast International Airport Constabulary, for example, was established under the Aerodromes Act (Northern Ireland) 1971 and the Airport (Northern Ireland) Order 1994. The Mersey Tunnels Police are sworn in as constables under s. 105 of the County of Merseyside Act 1981 as amended by the Local Government Act 1985. Those bodies that fit this category of policing organisation are listed in Table 5.1, together with their statutory undertaker, the year of their establishment, current legislation affecting them and their strength.

Most ports police organisations carry out duties that are the responsibility of security officers at other, comparable ports. Indeed, some large ports (such as Southampton) manage to police their property adequately without recourse to a special police organisation. The opinion that they are there to counter drug smuggling and illegal immigration is misguided as these duties are still the responsibility of HM Customs and Excise and the Immigration and Nationality Directorate. In most ports the officers' powers are confined to the port and one mile beyond. The main functions of these organisations are to carry out access control duties both in and out of the port, to prevent thefts, to enforce traffic regulations and generally to maintain order. The 1994 annual report of the Dover Harbour Board Police (DHBP) recorded 1,191 crimes, of which the most significant group was 488 thefts from shops onboard ferries. Other crimes included 59 thefts from vehicles, 19 cases of actual bodily harm, 13 cases of unlawful possession of a firearm, 2 cases of the possession of an offensive weapon and 1 bomb hoax. Hence the main problem this force faces is property crime. In 1994 the DHBP had an establishment of 52 constables and 19 civilians (the 2000 *Police Almanac* states 51 and 26 respectively) headed by a Chief Superintendent and a rank structure similar to that of a Home Office constabulary. New recruits receive four weeks' induction training, and attend various specialist courses run by other police organisations. The DHBP also has access to the police national computer.

Most ports police constables are not subject to the same accountability mechanisms as their Home Office counterparts. Section 96 of the Police and Criminal Evidence Act 1984 provides for the establishment for a body of constables (other than those maintained by a police authority) and for the establishment of a complaints and discipline procedure agreed between the authority maintaining the force and the PCA, subject to the approval of the Secretary of State. The Secretary of State also has the power to impose these procedures after consultation with the PCA and the authority maintaining the force. So far in England and Wales only the Port of London Authority Police and Port of Liverpool Police have complied with this (Department of Transport 1990; Police Complaints Authority 1995). Hence the mechanisms for complaints against constables for the remaining organisations lie outside the control of the PCA.

The status of some of these organisations has been further blurred with the privatisation of many of the ports. The ports of London, Tees and Hartlepool, Liverpool and Felixstowe have all been privatised in recent years. This has created the situation where private companies now effectively run their own private police organisations that still have constabulary powers. In theory the constables still retain their independence, but it seems unlikely the police organisations they work for would pursue objectives that differed significantly from those of their paymasters. This raises, therefore, questions about independence and accountability.

Not surprisingly, ports police have been the subject of government interest in recent years. In 1990 the Department of Transport issued a consultation paper on their future. This followed the decision by Sealink at Parkeston Quay to end its use of the BTP and, instead, to swear in private security officers as special constables. The study (Department of Transport 1990: 10) concluded there was no longer any justification for members of port police organisations to have full constabulary powers: 'Small private police forces do not have the size or facilities to ensure that constables are as highly trained as their counterparts in local county forces, nor are they accountable in the same way for the exercise of their constabulary powers.' The future of these organisations seems to be one of gradual extinction. In recent years Milford Haven Port Police has been replaced by security officers. The numbers of personnel employed by the Port of Tilbury Police have fallen from nearly 300 in the late 1970s, to 47 in 1988 and to around 25 in 2000. Similar trends have occurred across most of the other police organisations. It seems unlikely, given the government's attitude to these organisations and the expense of maintaining them vis-à-vis private security, that new police constabularies will be created. Those already established will either be gradually phased out or will decrease in size of establishment.

Chapter 6

Non-private security private policing bodies

There are number of organisations engaged in policing that display the characteristics of 'privateness', but which, for various reasons, cannot be classified as private security organisations. These bodies are often ignored when the spectrum of organisations involved in policing is explored (the classification of policing developed by Jones and Newburn (1998) for example, did not include this category). Some of these organisations, however, have high public profiles and engage in important functions. This chapter, therefore, considers these bodies along similar lines to those used in previous chapters.

Protecting the public and animals

A number of private organisations have emerged to protect the public and animals. Perhaps the best known of these is the RSPCA, which can trace its origins back to 1824 (that is, before the formation of the modern police in 1829) (Royal Society for the Prevention of Cruelty to Animals 2001). The RSPCA is a private charitable organisation that obtains its resources from donations given by the public and its members. One of its functions is to operate as a public police force, as members of the public can report allegations of cruelty to the charity, who will usually then investigate them. If evidence of a crime against an animal is found, the RSPCA will initiate its own prosecution. It might, therefore, be useful at this point to explore some of the activities of the RSPCA in some depth.

The RSPCA has an inspectorate of 328 individuals who pursue five main areas of work. First are situations where an allegation of cruelty against an animal has been made by a member of the public, which is then investigated. Secondly are prosecutions for cruelty to animals where the RSPCA establishes a prima facie case and proceedings are instigated against the perpetrator(s). Thirdly are rescues where inspectors rescue trapped animals or those in a situation they cannot extricate themselves from. Fourthly are collections of unowned and/or injured animals which are taken to a vet, home or clinic. Finally are inspections of circuses, livestock markets and zoos etc. Clearly, some of the inspectorate's work is not a form of policing but the investigation, inspection and prosecution work it undertakes warrants classifying the RSPCA as a policing body. The BBC television series the *Animal Police* (broadcast in 2000) revealed the full spectrum of RSPCA activities, from the investigation of cruelty to pet dogs to the neglect of whole herds of animals on farms. These investigations range from simple visits to homes to the pursuit of complex undercover investigations. For instance, in Portsmouth in 2000, the Special Operations Unit of the RSPCA was involved in an undercover investigation into at least 15 men alleged to be involved in organising illegal dog-fighting (Vaughan 2000). Twelve years previously, two men in Portsmouth had been prosecuted by the RSPCA for this offence, for which they both received the maximum 180 days in prison. This example graphically illustrates the policing activities of the RSPCA. The statistics in the Table 6.1, however, illustrate how large a role the RSPCA plays in policing animal crime in England and Wales. Indeed, in 1999 expenditure on prosecutions and operational support amounted to nearly £27 million, almost half the RSPCA's budget (RSPCA 2000).

Table 6.1 The workload of the RSPCA inspectorate

	1999	1998
Phone calls received	1,572,344	1,558,131
Cruelty complaints investigated	132,021	124,374
Establishments inspected	15,708	16,941
Prosecutions	701	853
Convictions	2,791	3,144
Defendants	970	1,125

Source: RSPCA (2000).

RSPCA inspectors undergo intensive training, including a 23-week course that covers welfare legislation, investigative procedures, legal issues, veterinary issues and even rope, ladder, boat and abseil training. The inspectors (with their police-like uniforms) are often considered to be an extension of the public police. While they possess no special statutory powers they do, on many occasions, work alongside police officers.

In Scotland, the Scottish Society for the Prevention of Cruelty to Animals (SSPCA – founded in 1839) pursues a similar range of activities as the RSPCA. It has an inspectorate of 55 individuals with 8 auxillaries (Scottish Society for the Prevention of Cruelty to Animals 2001). In the more specific area of birds, the Royal Society for the Protection of Birds (RSPB) similarly performs some policing roles. However, this organisation has fewer resources than the RSPCA, having only a couple of inspectors and rarely undertakes private prosecutions. Indeed, the last time the RSPB pursued a prosecution was in 1992. It prefers instead to assist the Crown Prosecution Service (CPS) and Procurator Fiscal in preparing a case (Royal Society for the Protection of Birds Investigations Section 1999).

The NSPCC (like the RSPCA) is a charitable organisation founded in the nineteenth century (1884) but with the goal of protecting children (National Society for the Prevention of Cruelty to Children 2000). However, while the RSPCA has emerged as the primary policing agency in its sphere of work, the NSPCC is but one of many organisations involved with the prevention of cruelty to children: it is the police and the social services departments of local authorities who play the most significant roles.

The NSPCC exists to prevent children suffering from cruelty; to protect those who are at risk of harm; to help children who have suffered harm overcome the effects of that harm; and to work to protect children from further harm (National Society for the Prevention of Cruelty to Children 2001). To achieve these aims the NSPCC (like the RSPCA) has a 24-hour help-line where the public can report concerns or make complaints. This help-line receives over 49,000 calls per year. The NSPCC also has over 180 teams located throughout the country who undertake a range of tasks, one of which is the investigation of allegations of child abuse (National Society for the Prevention of Cruelty to Children 2000). Other activities include campaigning and counselling and educational and preventative projects. A case typical of the work of the NSPCC was cited in its 1999 annual report (ibid.). Susan had met a friend in an Internet chat room who was in fact a middle-aged man. The 'friendship' progressed and the man began to make sexual suggestions, threatening to stalk Susan if she broke off the relationship. Her mother phoned the NSPCC help-line and the counsellor referred the case to the local police and social services, who worked with the NSPCC in investigating the case.

As in any activity where large sums of money at stake, frauds may arise – and horse racing has not escaped this (Onslow 1992). To protect the public and to regulate horse racing, the Jockey Club was established. This club has a Security Department whose functions include preventing the use of prohibited substances, crime and malpractice and liaising with the local police to achieve these objectives. (This could be regarded as an in-house security department but, as its aims include protecting the public, it was considered appropriate to include it in this section.) Despite having no special statutory status, the officers employed by this department have an impressive range of powers. Controversially, the Security Department recently awarded itself powers to demand access to jockeys' and trainers' personal documents, such as telephone bills, betting accounts, etc. Failure to agree to supply these could result in a fine or even a ban (Wood 2000). The Security Department has a full-time staff of 44, supplemented by 90 part-time staff, and it has an annual budget of £2 million (Cooper 1997). It undertakes surveillance at every race course, monitors every race and stable and tests over 7,500 horses each year.

Protecting organisations' revenue

Many policing organisations have been created to protect the revenues of certain industries and sectors of commerce. These have been established because of a lack of interest from the police in such matters and because highly specialised skills are needed to undertake this kind of investigation.

A wide variety of products are illegally copied and/or counterfeited. Computer software, compact disks, videos, etc., are just some examples of where copyright and other legislation are breached. This type of crime is often a low priority for the police and for other public law-enforcement bodies, such as the trading standards service. As noted above, it is also a crime that often requires specialist skills and expertise if it is to be investigated effectively. Hence some sectors of industry have developed their own policing infrastructures to prevent such crime, to identify problem areas, to conduct investigations and to liaise with other policing agencies.

The Federation against Software Theft (FAST) is a non-profit-making organisation funded by the computer industry. For example, FAST investigators work closely with trading standards officers and the police. For example, in June 1998 FAST, trading standards and the police conducted raids on an address in Wolverhampton that resulted in five arrests and the seizure of over £1 million worth of counterfeit software. In another case in Kingston in July 1999, Terence Brown was convicted on nine counts of copyright and trademark offences after having been found to be pirating computer software. He was sentenced to two years' imprisonment. This conviction followed an investigation by FAST and Kingston Trading Standards. In 1997 alone, FAST seized £78 million worth of pirated software, which illustrates the extent and success of their operations (Federation against Software Theft 2001). In the field of films, television and video, the Federation against Copyright Theft (FACT) is an investigative organisation funded by the British and American film, video and television industries. It has 10 investigators (mostly ex-police officers). In the case of copyright and trademark infringements in the music industry, the investigative body is the Music Publishers Association (MPA). All three organisations have come together in recent years, however, to fund an integrated piracy hotline that provides a single point of contact for the public, for law enforcement agencies and for Internet and other creative industries to obtain information on film, music and software copyright issues.

In the UK the state-broadcasting organisation, the BBC, is largely funded by revenue raised through a TV licence. Everyone who owns a television must possess a licence, and failure to do so could result in prosecution with a fine of up to £1,000. Under the Broadcasting Act 1990, the BBC was given responsibility for licence administration and, in 1998, the BBC contracted out its licensing functions to Envision (a consortium of Bull Information Systems and the Post Office) under a seven-year contract (BBC press notice, 27 October 1998). Envision operates under the trading name 'TV Licensing'. It administers the database of licence-holders, sends reminders, processes queries, applications and payments and searches for those who haven't purchased a licence. Envision employs over 1,700 staff and catches on average 1,000 people a day who do not have a TV licence, many of whom are prosecuted in the courts (TV Licensing 2001). This is thus an example of a public organisation that has contracted out its revenue protection activities to a private company who are engaged in investigations and prosecutions.

There are also some international bodies that undertake similar work. The International Chamber of Commerce (ICC), for example, is a world business organisation that promotes its member companies' and associations' interests overseas (ICC 2001). The ICC has a commercial crime service (ICCCCS) that has five subdivisions (ICC Commercial Crime Services 2001). These subdivisions are the International Maritime Bureau (IMB), the Commercial Crime Bureau (CCB), the Counterfeiting

Intelligence Bureau (CIB), the Cybercrime Unit and the IMB Piracy Reporting Centre. The activities of these organisations warrant a great deal of further research, particularly given the huge increase in globalisation. All it is possible to do here, however, is to give a brief overview of some of their work.

The IMB (founded in 1981), has roles that include preventing fraud in international trade and maritime transport, reducing the risk of piracy and assisting law enforcement agencies in protecting crews. While much of the bureau's work concerns the prevention of crime, it also conducts investigations with the aim of bringing fraudsters to justice (International Chamber of Commerce International Maritime Bureau 2001). The problem of piracy led the ICC to create the IMB Piracy Reporting Centre, which is involved solely in tackling the growing problem of piracy. This centre provides its members with intelligence on the risk of piracy so they can take the most appropriate decisions to reduce the risk. The CCB was set up in 1992 to provide services to banks and financial companies to help them prevent frauds. It provides monthly reports to members on risks and on the nature of frauds, amongst other things. It also authenticates documents, analyses financial transactions, vets companies, traces and recovers assets, provides expert testimony in courts and organises training sessions and seminars (ICC Commercial Crime Bureau 2001). Counterfeiting has also become a problem for businesses worldwide. To address this pattern, in 1985 the ICC founded the CIB. This bureau gathers and evaluates intelligence on counterfeiting; investigates the sources and distribution of such goods; provides advice and training; and works with the police to make arrests and to seize counterfeit goods (ICC Counterfeiting Intelligence Bureau 2001). The final and most recent subdivision is the Cybercrime Unit, which was established in 1999. This unit tracks the methods used by criminals to perpetrate crimes on the Internet; provides advice on security information systems; disseminates intelligence; and works with law enforcement agencies to combat this problem (ICC Cybercrime Unit 2001). Together these different subdivisions of the ICC amount to a specialised and sophisticated international private policing body for the international business community.

Enforcing the decisions of the courts

The courts of England and Wales employ publicly appointed officers to enforce their decisions, and these officers have special powers. In the high court these officers are contracted by the state. High court under-sheriffs enforce high court warrants. Under these Warrants, under-sheriffs have the power to seize goods, to sell them, to restore goods to their rightful owners and to take possession – by force if necessary – of buildings and land (Gladwin 1974). Recently their work has come to national notice as a result of environmental protests, such as that at Newbury. At these protests, the under-sheriffs were charged with the responsibility of executing a series of writs for the possession of the land for the Secretary of State for Transport, amongst other interested parties (Button *et al* 2001). Under-sheriffs and their officers have the power to use reasonable force to execute a writ of possession. The under-sheriff is usually a solicitor appointed by the High Sheriff and he or she charges a fee for this work (Button and John forthcoming). The officers are sworn in as sheriff's officers, which gives them special powers. The officers are usually individuals who normally in other occupations (in the case of environment protests, for example, as tree surgeons), and they receive their fees from the under-sheriff via the paying client. At county court level there are county court bailiffs who have similar roles and powers to sheriff's officers but who are directly employed by the courts.

Chapter 7

Voluntary policing

This chapter considers some of the many individuals and organisations involved in policing but in a voluntary capacity. Johnston (1992a) divided voluntary policing into two categories: 'responsible citizenship' and 'autonomous citizenship'. The criteria he uses to make this distinction are based on whether the policing activity concerned is sanctioned by the state or not. This chapter, therefore, begins by looking at some of the many voluntary activities that are sanctioned (and often encouraged) by the state. These activities include such things as joining police reserves in a voluntary capacity and participating in Neighbourhood Watch, to some of the activities the media and other organisations partake in to support policing. The chapter then goes on to examine some of the many individuals and organisations that do not have the sanction of the state. These vary from spontaneous acts of vigilantism to more organised forms of policing. The chapter also considers Johnston's (1996) criminological assessment of what vigilantism is and it explores those things that have caused vigilantism to emerge.

Responsible citizenship

'Responsible citizenship' covers a wide range of activities. At one level it might be phoning the police after witnessing a suspicious activity or, at another, joining the special constabulary. The most important thing about this type of policing is that it has the official sanction of the state. The most notable forms of responsible citizenship in the UK are membership of the special constabulary and involvement with the local Neighbourhood

Watch. It is not, however, simply individual citizens who contribute to voluntary policing: organisations are also involved. Private companies, for instance, often donate money and resources to voluntary policing activities, as do some charities. The media may also help by publicising voluntary activities, as well as by investigating crimes themselves. These activities often have the official sanction of the state.

Volunteer police

One of the most common forms of responsible citizenship in the UK and many other countries is citizens who give up some of their spare time to undertake policing duties, usually as auxiliaries to the full-time police. These volunteers usually come within the official command structure of the police. In the USA, there is a variety of ways in which volunteers can contribute, and these vary between jurisdictions. In St Louis the reserve have full police powers and are armed. In New York, however, they do not have any special powers (Johnston 1992a). In the UK, the voluntary police is the special constabulary of the local constabulary. These volunteers are the direct descendants of parish constables. Special constables wear almost identical uniforms to their full-time colleagues, hold the same powers (although restricted to the constabulary area) and, in some cases, carry out a range of duties similar to those of full-time constables. In the Metropolitan Police Service (MPS), for instance, specials are involved in providing specialist crime-prevention advice and in teaching women self-defence. In most constabularies, special constables do basic patrol work and they police large-scale public events, such as football matches and demonstrations.

Research by Leon (1989) found that 54 per cent of specials undertake at least four duties (taking 4–8 hours in total) each month. However, 40 per cent pursued only one duty every two to three weeks. At the other extreme, 4 per cent undertook four duties each week. Training also varies considerably between forces as it must meet the needs of each individual constabulary. According to research conducted by Gill (1987), the training given is similar to that given to regular officers. However, Leon's (1989) research suggests this might be changing as large numbers of teenagers are new joining the specials from different professional backgrounds. Recent Home Office data estimates there are over 18,000 special constables in England and Wales (although in 1946 there were nearly 120,000). There is, generally, a high level of turnover and there have been a number of unsuccessful campaigns to try to improve recruitment.

The special constabulary's future raises a number of issues. For example, the Home Office is keen to expand it for a number of reasons: first, the special constabulary enables costs to be reduced and secondly, it is regarded as positive force bridging the gap between the police and the community. A further issue concerns the role of special constables. The Police Federation, for example, has expressed concerns about the 'creeping' use of the special constabulary to replace regular officers in 'soft' policing roles, thus creating some form of two-tier policing.

Some constabularies have created schemes whereby volunteers can help the police but without becoming special constables. In 1996 a police station staffed by 15 unpaid volunteers was established in Southwater, West Sussex, to deal with inquiries, lost property and the filling out of crime reports. This scheme permitted the villagers to have access to a police station for a greater period of time, and it also enabled the officers to dedicate more time to patrolling (McCartney 1996).

Some countries, when faced with a crisis, draw upon the support of volunteers. This is sometimes done for the more politically motivated aim of maintaining power but is also often a reflection of a state's genuine concern over the disorder. Some authoritarian regimes, for example, frequently make use of these types of volunteers. In Cuba during the early 1960s, the fear of counter-revolutionary activities led to the establishment of the 'Committees for the Defense of the Revolution', which mobilised thousands of citizens into action (Kowalewski 1982). In the Soviet Union during the Khrushchev era, the voluntary militia (or *druzhiny*) was formed as volunteer brigades to support the state militia. Their primary role was to maintain public order and they wore distinctive red arm-bands and lapel pins.

It is not only authoritarian regimes, however, that have resorted to these measures. In the aftermath of the First World War in the UK, there was fear amongst the governing classes of unrest amongst the working classes. One of the responses to this fear was the encouragement of local constabularies to maintain special constables. During the General Strike of 1926 there was an appeal for volunteers to supplement the special constabulary, and the state entered the dispute by supplying 226,000 special constables (Bunyan 1976). This type of measure has frequently been termed 'state-sponsored vigilantism' (Kowalewski 1982, 1996). As is shown later in this chapter, however, one of the most important components of vigilantism is that it is 'autonomous': it does not have the sanction of the state. As the type of activity described here clearly does have the sanction of the state, the term 'vigilantism' cannot be used to describe it.

Neighbourhood Watch

The most noticeable form of responsible citizenship in the UK is membership of a Neighbourhood Watch scheme. Under these schemes, local communities become more involved in the surveillance of their localities and report suspicious activities to the police (Johnston 1992a). Local police officers are also assigned to the schemes to try to improve links between the community and the police. Neighbourhood Watch has been very successful in terms of numbers participating. From the first scheme established in 1982, in 1996 there were over 147,000 schemes in operation (Gilling 1997). Despite their popularity and the apparent firm support from the police, there is mixed evidence about their effectiveness. Bennett (1990), in his assessment of neighbourhood watch schemes, found no positive effects as a result of the schemes in terms of the level of crime or the fear of crime. He argued that, ultimately, the level of public surveillance is limited because most domestic properties are empty during the day and/or because people have but limited opportunities to participte in surveillance. His research also cast doubt on offenders being deterred by such schemes. There were, however, positive benefits in terms of improving community/police relations.

Spontaneous citizen involvement

When crimes are committed, the state expects the citizens who have witnessed them to respond in a suitable manner. A suitable manner means calling the police, acting as a witness or, sometimes, apprehending the offender. Bystander involvement in policing has been the subject of much US research. Smith and Visher (1981) found that bystanders were already present at over 50 per cent of cases of misdemeanour and felony by the time the police arrived. However, the response the police would like from potential witnesses was not always forthcoming.

Shotland and Goodstein (1984) identified four types of bystander behaviour, some of which would not have received the state's support. The first response they identified was 'non-intervention', where bystanders do not get involved in an incident. This might mean either fleeing the scene or simply not responding to the crime. Shotland and Goodstein (ibid.) give the example of a woman who was raped in front of 25 roofing-company employees, who failed to answer her screams for help – they thought she was having an argument with her boyfriend. Shotland and Stebbins (1980) conducted further research into this type of bystander behaviour. These researchers simulated a rape scene: bystanders saw what they thought was a woman been dragged into a room, followed by a loud verbal exchange between the woman and her 'attacker'. Of those bystanders who witnessed the incident, only 68 per cent responded to what they had seen and heard. Moreover, only 13 per cent tried to intervene when they heard the shouting.

The next category identified by Shotland and Goodstein (1984) is 'indirect intervention', where bystanders intervene *after* the incident. This might involve telephoning the police after witnessing a crime to give a description of the assailant. This type of behaviour is the bare minimum the state would expect from a citizen, and bystanders frequently decide not to become directly involved in a crime, not least because of the dangers they see this course of action might put them in.

Following on from this category is 'direct intervention', where bystanders intervene directly to disrupt the crime. This usually means protecting the victim by confronting the perpetrator in an attempt to apprehend him or her. The police are 'wary' about this type of behaviour ('have-a-go-heroes'). The state would generally only support such action where there was no risk to the citizen. In the final category ('spontaneous vigilantism'), the bystander not only apprehends the offender but also delivers the punishment. This type of behaviour is not generally supported by the state and is explored in greater depth below under the heading 'Autonomous citizenship'.

The media

The media can become involved in policing in two ways. First it can publicise crimes in an attempt to secure information about those who may have committed them. Secondly, some journalists become involved themselves in the investigation of crime. The best known example in the UK of this first form of media involvement is the BBC television programme *Crimewatch UK* (Johnston 1992a). This programme highlights particular crimes, using witnesses, the police and, sometimes, victims, to appeal for information. The crimes are often re-enacted in attempt to 'jog' the memories of those viewers who may have witnessed the crime and may know personally those people who committed the crime. Rewards are often offered for 'information leading to the arrest and conviction' of the perpetrators. This programme has a large audience and generally focuses on the more spectacular crimes, such as murders, rapes, armed robberies, etc. A wide range of other television programmes also appeal for information about crimes, at both a national and regional level. Both the radio and newspapers make appeals for information about crimes and, finally the Internet is also increasingly being used in this way. The Federal Bureau of Investigation (FBI) has a website containing its 'most wanted' criminals, as does Interpol (see http://www.fbi.gov/mostwant/topten/tenlist.htm).

Many television programmes and journalists investigate criminal behaviour. These include investigations into alleged criminals as well as investigations into alleged criminal behaviour by police officers, politicians and other public figures. Some of the television programmes that undertake such activities include *The Cook Report, World in Action, Panorama* and *Dispatches*. In such programmes, criminal behaviour is often exposed and the programme makers then pass on the information they have to the police for further investigation. *The Cook Report,* for example, has investigated, among other things, Irish terrorism, major fraud, drug dealers and plutonium smugglers (Cook 1999). In many ways this could be considered 'hybrid' policing because of the organised nature of the investigations and because of the paid 'investigators' and researchers who conduct them. However, the investigators are paid primarily to produce a television programme rather than to investigate a crime, and so their contribution to policing is considered here to be voluntary.

Private companies and charities

One of the more common ways by which private companies and charities become involved in policing is through the provision of funds to promote crime prevention projects (Johnston 1992a). In 1989, for example, the Royal Insurance group donated £100,000 worth of property-marking kits to Neighbourhood Watch schemes, and Woolworths has, in the past, donated money to Crime Concern. While it is not possible here to discuss all the activities private companies and charities have been involved in, one scheme that does deserve more consideration is 'Crimestoppers'. Crimestoppers (which began life in the USA) relies on co-operation between the business community, the police and the public. The scheme operates in the following way. A crime that has been targeted for attention is highlighted in the media and the public are invited to phone in anonymously with any information they can provide about the crime. If this information leads to an arrest, the informant can apply for a reward without jeopardising his or her anonymity. A large number of criminals have been arrested as a result of this scheme. In 1996, for example, 4,347 arrests were made as a result of information received (Crimestoppers Trust 1997). An example of such an arrest is given in the trust's 1996 annual review. As a result of appeals made in the press for information concerning the crime, a 19-year-old who had raped a young girl was arrested, charged and sentenced to 10 years' imprisonment. The person who had supplied the information that led to this person's arrest donated his £10,000 reward to the victim (Crimestoppers Trust 1997).

Such schemes, however, are not without their critics. In Canada, for example, critics have arued that Crimestoppers enables a 'deviance-defining elite' to shape public perceptions about crime and the fear of crime (Carriere and Erikson 1989). In the UK concerns have been raised about the trust's focus on high-profile but infrequent crimes, such as rape, murder and armed robbery.

Autonomous citizenship

Personal vengeance is one of the oldest – if not the oldest – forms of policing. Often referred to as vigilantism, this type of policing involves an individual or group of citizens taking out its revenge against a known or alleged offender. It also includes more organised forms of voluntary policing, such as citizens patrolling the streets to maintain law and order.

Spontaneous self-policing

Acts of spontaneous self-policing (or spontaneous vigilantism, as Shotland and Goodstein (1984) describe it) are frequently undertaken by individuals who know or believe a person or organisation has committed a crime against them and who then go on to punish the alleged perpetrator through an act of violence. The release of convicted paedophiles into the community, for example, has led, in some cases, to groups of residents attempting to drive such people out of their areas. These measures frequently involve acts of violence and intimidation. While such extreme examples of self-policing are not usually tolerated by society at large, there are bystander actions that are tolerated and, indeed, encouraged by the state.

Vigilantism

Despite the high profile often given to acts of vigilantism, criminologists have generally paid little attention to it. Much of the literature concerning vigilantism, therefore, comes from political scientists (Rosenbaum and Sedeberg 1976) and anthropologists (Abrahams 1998). The literature that does exist, however, has not grappled seriously with the question about the meaning of the term vigilantism. It is not surprising, therefore, that almost any act to combat criminal behaviour is usually labelled 'vigilantism'. To address this problem of definition, Johnston (1996) identified what he considered to be the six essential characteristics of vigilantism.

The first characteristic of vigilantism Johnston (ibid.) identified is that vigilantism involves some form of planning, premeditation or organisation. While this might appear to rule out spontaneous acts of vigilantism, this planning has only to be minimal – as little as setting traps to catch a burglar. Tony Martin, the Norfolk man who shot and killed a 16-year-old, was alleged to have set traps and lookout positions on his farm to catch burglars. He also had a pump-action action shot gun to protect himself, despite having been banned from holding such weapons. The Tony Martin case illustrates quite clearly how the British criminal justice system treats such incidents. Despite being heralded a 'hero' in some quarters, Martin was found guilty of murder and sentenced to life imprisonment (Judd 2000). In another case, however, Stephen Owen was acquitted of shooting the man who had knocked down and killed his son. The driver had no licence and a string of motoring convictions and was sentenced to only 6 months' imprisonment for killing Owen's son (Johnston 1996).

Johnston's second characteristic of vigilantism is that it is a private, voluntary act. This begs the question as to whether an act of policing perpetrated by an off-duty police officer counts as an act of vigilantism (Rosenbaum and Sedeberg 1976) – did the off-duty police officer undertake the policing as an individual or as an agent of the state? (Police officers usually retain their powers when off duty.) If police officers commit acts that could be considered illegitimate (i.e. they are acting as individuals rather than agents of the state), Johnston suggests, then should these acts be considered illegal actions of state officials rather than vigilantism?

The third element Johnston identifies is that vigilantism must be autonomous: it must have no support or authority from the state. If this is the case, all forms of vigilantism must be condemned by the state (even less extreme examples of vigilantism, such as the Guardian Angels, which are discussed later in this chapter). Johnston's fourth characteristic is that vigilantism must also use, or threaten to use, force. As is illustrated later in this chapter, paramilitaries in Northern Ireland frequently assassinate members of their community for what they consider to be 'deviant acts'. Violence, however, might simply be threatened: citizen patrols in Balsall Heath, Birmingham, with the intention of driving prostitutes and their customers out of the area, were alleged to have made threats of violence. One prostitute received a note through her door that said: 'HELLO BITCH – we could smash your windows, we could smash your face – best of all, we could burn you out … like they say, you would make nice crackling' (cited in Mills 1998: 7).

The fifth characteristic of vigilantism is that it is a reaction to crime and perceived social deviance. Brown (1975), writing about the USA of the nineteenth century, distinguished 'classic' vigilantism (such as actions taken against horse thieves, outlaws and the rural lower classes) from 'neo-vigilantism' (actions taken against urban Catholics, negroes and union leaders). Classic vigilantism encompasses crime control whereas neo-vigilantism involves 'social control'. Silke (1998), in assessing the vigilante activities of Irish paramilitaries, distinguished anti-social acts (such as theft, burglary, etc.) from anti-paramilitary acts (such as informing, associating with the security forces and refusing to pay protection money). The boundaries become blurred here, however. While the primary aim of kneecapping a youth might be political, punishing a 'joy-rider' for 'anti-social behaviour' could also have political overtones. Johnston (1996), however, does not exclude reacting to social deviance from his typology because many social control functions ultimately have an anti-criminal intent. Cohen (1985), on the other hand, has argued that social control is in danger of becoming a 'Mickey Mouse' concept because of its ubiquitous use: using social control as an umbrella term to encompass things other than social deviance makes the term so wide in meaning as to be unwieldly.

Finally, Johnston's sixth characteristic of vigilantism is that it must contribute to a personal or collective sense of security. This means a vigilante action must have a purpose beyond dealing with a specific act of deviance to contribute towards a greater personal or collective 'security'. Much has been written about the increasing needs for basic levels of security among citizens (e.g. Spitzer 1987; Loader 1997) and about the rise of vigilante action should these needs not be met by the state.

The conditions that make vigilantism likely

This section looks at some factors that might give rise to vigilantism. It is not suggested, however, that all these factors are necessary for vigilantism to occur or that, if they exist, vigilantism will inevitably arise. These are, rather, factors commonly associated with vigilantism.

The most important of these factors is the perception the criminal justice system is not addressing specific or general criminal behaviour effectively. Whether this perception is based upon reality or not varies between places and from one time to another. For instance, the emergence of vigilantism in the USA during the nineteenth century in the mid-western states was largely because there was hardly any criminal justice system and because that which did exist was extremely inefficient (Abrahams 1998). Such was the pace of development in these 'virgin' lands the state could not keep up. Consequently, when crime and other social problems arose it was often impossible for the local agents of policing to combat them and so the citizens often took the law 'into their own hands'. In the UK, although there is an established, strong criminal justice system, there have been times when the response of 'the system' to certain crimes and police concerns has not matched public expectations.

The vigilantism in Paulsgrove, Portsmouth, during the Summer of 2000 was based upon a perception by the residents of this area, that the criminal justice system was not doing enough to police and punish paedophiles.

Acts of vigilantism may also be sparked off by a sensational crime that captures an individual's or group's imagination. Again, in the Paulsgrove example given above, interest in paedophiles during the summer of 2000 was sparked off by the murder of a young girl, Sarah Payne, by Roy Whiting. In the aftermath of this tragic event, Sarah's parents began a campaign for a public register of paedophiles. This led to the *News of the World* printing the names and locations of known paedophiles. This action by the newspaper was a major contributory factor to some of the residents of the area taking more of an interest in some of the males who lived on their estate and campaigning to have them removed.

A further factor relates to a community's social and ethnic homogeneity communities (Shotland and Goodstein 1984). If the people living in a community have the same social and ethnic background, they will tend to share the same values, will trust each other and will communicate with each other freely. This facilitates the identification, pursuit and punishment of offenders. Common social bonds have also been identified in the literature that seeks to explain the rise of mass social movements (Klandermans 1997).

The final factor that can contribute to vigilantism (and as highlighted by Johnston (1996)) is leadership and organisation. While the degrees of organisation and planning acts of vigilantism require vary, ultimately a degree of leadership is necessary to take the initiative forward and to plan the act.

The range of vigilante action

The range of vigilante activity varies, from individuals with few skills or little experience to highly organised paramilitaries.

The lone vigilante

Perhaps the most famous example in recent years of the lone vigilante is the Norfolk farmer, Tony Martin. Martin had been the target of a number of burglaries and had become increasingly agitated by the problem. To combat this, he was alleged to have set up lookouts throughout his farm so he could keep vulnerable locations under surveillance, to have set gaps in his stairs as 'booby-traps' and to have slept in his clothes with his illegal gun by his side. One night when two burglars broke into his farmhouse, Martin killed one and shot the other in the legs. He was found guilty of murder and sentenced to life imprisonment (Judd 2000).

Group vigilantism: semi-organised

There have been many examples of vigilantism pursued by groups of people with little organisational structure. One such example was the deployment of patrols by local residents in Balsall Heath, Birmingham during the 1990s to combat the growing problem of prostitutes working on the streets. The area had become an Amsterdam-like haven for prostitutes and their clients, with some homes in the area having red lights and with prostitutes sitting in the windows. The residents (many of whom were Asians with deep religious objections to this trade) organised patrols to drive the clients and prostitutes out of their area. Their campaign was largely successful but it received mixed support from the police because of the tactics used (physical threats, harassment and zealously questioning any strangers who entered the area, amongst other things) (Mills 1998). The example of the vigilante campaign in Paulsgrove, Portsmouth, against alleged paedophiles, as described earlier in this chapter, would also fit this category.

Group vigilantism: organised

Perhaps one of the best known international organisations that could be considered a vigilante group is the Guardian Angels, whose activities are often opposed by the police. Originally from the USA, they arrived in the UK in 1989 and now have 80 chapters in London, Manchester and Nottingham. These volunteer policing agents wear a uniform comprising a sweatshirt and red beret, and they spend their time riding on trains and patrolling public areas (Wheelwright 1998).

While there has been little research into the Guardian Angels in the UK, there has been much interest shown in them in the USA. In one study carried out in New York in the early 1980s (Ostrowe and DiBiase 1983), subway passengers were asked for their opinions about the transit police and the New York Police Department (NYPD) and the Guardian Angels. The research showed that most people (61 per cent) wanted to see more Guardian Angels patrolling the subway than transit police (13 per cent) or NYPD officers (12 per cent) (ibid.). The same research also found that only 4 per cent of respondents opposed the Angels, compared to 43 per cent who were opposed to the transit police and 52 per cent who were opposed to NYPD officers.

In Northern Ireland, paramilitaries have emerged as the main form of policing and punishment on some housing estates. This type of vigilantism occurs in both Republican and Loyalist communities, although for slightly different reasons (Silke 1999). The Provisional Irish Republican Army (PIRA) has been waging a terrorist campaign for over three decades to remove the British from Northern Ireland. In doing so it has evolved into an alternative criminal justice system, carrying out the functions of policing, investigation, trial and punishment. This has happened for a variety of reasons (Silke 1998). As the primary aim of the PIRA is to remove the British state and, thus, the British police from Northern Ireland, it has, in the mean time, to provide these basic state functions itself. The terrorist campaigns waged in Republican areas have forced the Royal Ulster Constabulary (RUC), to focus on 'counter-terrorism' rather than traditional crimes. This has enabled the PIRA to fill the gap in dealing with crime. To the people living in local communities it is considered dangerous to contact the RUC as there is a risk of being labelled an informer. Hence most people contact the PIRA about crime. Finally, many local residents approve of the punishments given out by the PIRA, and they often demand even harsher forms of punishment (ibid.). In Loyalist areas, on the other hand, the aim is not to remove the British state. The campaign against the Anglo-Irish Agreement in the mid-1980s, which had as its target members of the RUC, led to a policing vacuum the Loyalist paramilitaries were willing to fill. Such vigilantism not only enables these paramilitaries to exert control over their communities but it also permits them to detect informers in their communities (Silke 1999).

Having distinguished between the two major organisations involved in vigilantism in Northern Ireland, the nature of this vigilantism will now be examined. Most of this discussion relates to the PIRA because this is the most organised and sophisticated paramilitary group while some of the strategies described here also relate to the Loyalists there are differences, but these will not be explored here because of lack of space (those interested are referred to Silke 1999; Silke and Taylor 2000).

The PIRA polices both anti-social and anti-paramilitary acts. The latter involve such behaviour as informing, associating with political opponents or interfering in paramilitary activities. However, it is the former, anti-social acts (including such 'normal' crimes as car theft and joyriding, burglary, rape, child abuse, etc.) that are of greater interest here as these are unambiguously crimes that would normally be dealt with by the criminal justice system. Once a crime has been reported to the paramilitaries, they will decide whether the evidence is sufficient to punish the offender. Once this decision has been made, the type of punishment will be determined. Silke (1998) has identified eight forms of punishment that, in some respects, mirror the legitimate criminal justice system. These include: warnings, curfews, fines/victim restitution, acts of public humiliation, punishment beatings, punishment shootings, expulsions and assassinations. Some of these punishments are quite gruesome. For instance in one incident a 16-year-old boy was strapped upside down on railings and his legs were then beaten with baseball bats with nails embedded in them (*The Independent*, 27 March 1998).

While it is not possible to estimate the number and frequency of some of the 'lesser' punishments, those beatings and shootings that result in hospitalisation can be estimated. Silke (1998) suggests that, in three decades of vigilantism, at least 2,149 people have been subjected to punishment shootings, 1,328 to punishment beatings and around 114 have died as a result of attacks. Between 1994 and 1996, around 453 people were similarly subjected to PIRA expulsion orders.

It is not only terrorist groups who undertake policing activities outside the control of the state. Organised crime groups throughout the world have been known to undertake activities similar to Northern Ireland terrorist groups, alongside their own 'normal' criminal activities. Hobsbawn (1959), in his account of the Sicilian Mafia, illustrated how these groups of people became a de facto state, serving the interests of all in varying degrees. Chu (1996) describes how Hong Kong triads provide 'legitimate' policing services to the business community. There are numerous other examples of this type of policing activity in many countries of the world (see Burrows 1976; Rosenbaum and Sedeberg 1976; Johnston 1992a).

Chapter 8

The private security industry and policing

While the private security industry has received increased interest from both academics and policy-makers in recent years, it is still, however, a comparatively under-researched area (Reiner 2000a). This chapter, therefore, explores the growing role of the private security industry in policing. It begins by assessing the size of the industry and moves on to examine in more detail the activities of private security organisations involved in policing. It uses the examples of public order and investigative policing to illustrate this growth of private security firms. Before these issues are considered, however, it is important to establish what is meant by the term private security industry, as this term is open to very different interpretations and definitions.

What is the private security industry?

There has been a long debate in academic, legal, policy-making and industry circles over what constitutes private security (George and Button 2000). While there is not the space to rehearse these debates in depth here, it is important to distinguish the different sectors because some are very clearly engaged in policing, some are not, and yet others play a very ambiguous role. For instance, a CCTV system itself could be considered an instrument of policing but not the installer of that system. For the purposes of this book, the definition supplied by George and Button (2000: 15) will be used:

The term 'private security industry' is a generic term used to describe an amalgam of distinct industries and professions bound together by a number of functions, including crime prevention, order maintenance, loss reduction and protection; but these functions are neither common nor exclusive to all the activities of the private security industry, though the more that apply to a particular activity the more clearly it can be considered as private security. To be included within the industry, personnel must have a primarily security role, whether this is full-time or part-time, and there must also be an employment relationship, whether as an employee or self-employed. The industry also includes certain public sector security employees ... where their role is paralleled in the private security industry, the interest served is private and they hold no special statutory powers. The services and products of the private security industry are also generally categorised into a number of distinct sectors. There is also a large grey area around these sectors – and between them, in some cases – which we have called the 'margins' of the private security industry.

The distinct sectors George and Button identify include manned security services (static manned guarding, CIT services, door supervision and stewarding services, and close protection services); private sector detention services; security storage and destruction services; professional security services; and the security products sector. There are also at the margins of the industry a range of other activities, services and products.

The above is just one definition of the private security industry; other definitions have been attempted (see Draper 1978; Shearing and Stenning 1981; South 1988; Manunta 1999; George and Button 2000).

The size of the private security industry

The tremendous growth of the private security industry in Canada during the postwar period, together with the greater use of technology and management control systems in the public police led Stenning and Shearing (1980) to describe the changes that were taking place as a 'quiet revolution'. The same could be said of the British private security industry, but the size of the industry is still the subject of much academic debate. One thing, however, is clear: the industry has grown significantly in the postwar years, from a few specialised firms catering largely for the very rich to a multi-billion pound industry (South 1988; Jones and Newburn 1998).

Jones and Newburn (1998) estimated there were at least 6,900 security firms in Great Britain, employing 333,631 personnel. They arrived at the latter figure by multiplying the average number of employees per firm by the estimated total number of firms. George and Button (2000) used best estimates from all the sectors they considered to be part of the private security industry and arrived at a figure of 317,500 employees in an industry worth £5.5 billion. It would seem to safe to assume total employment in the private security industry is at least 300,000 employees, which means there are almost two security personnel for every one police officer. There could be substantially more employees than this, however, as the estimates of the number of door supervisors alone have ranged from 50,000 to 250,000 (Walker 1999), with 100,000 considered to be the most likely. Many security employees, on the other hand, are not directly engaged in policing as they manufacture and install locks and intruder alarms etc. Table 8.1 identifies the numbers of security personnel who have a *direct* policing role. These figures from (George and Button (2000: 30)), use some of the more conservative estimates of employee numbers (for door supervisors, for example).

Using the statistics given in this table, 1.4 security officers are engaged in policing to every one police officer (excluding non-Home Office police officers). While it is difficult to compare these figures with other countries because of differing definitions of what constitutes security staff and because of the different roles the police play in different jurisdictions, Cunningham et al (1990) estimated there were 2.6 security staff to every one police officer in the USA. In Canada the ratio was estimated to be two security officers to every one police officer (Campbell and Reingold 1994) and, in Australia, 1.5 security officers to every one police officer (Reynolds and Wilson 1997).

Using the factors identified by George and Button (2000), it might be useful here to outline the causes of the growth in the private security industry. The most important cause they identify is a growth both in crime itself and of the fear of crime. This has led individuals and organisations to seek greater protection. A further cause is the growth of terrorism, which has led to increases in demand for security out of all proportion to the risk involved (Cunningham et al 1990). The rise in the number of protests and demonstrations has had a similar effect. George and Button (2000) also demonstrate how insurance companies often demand specific security arrangements are in place before agreeing to supply cover or to grant discounts. The privatisation of parts of the criminal justice system has also led to increasing opportunities for the private security industry, as has the inability of the government to fund the police in line with the increasing demands placed upon the service.

Table 8.1 Total number of security personnel engaged in policing in the UK

Category	Number
Private security personnel directly engaged in policing	
Security officers	140,000
Door supervisors	50,000
Stewards	12,000
Professional investigators	15,000
Total	**217,000**
Police officers (excluding non-Home Office police officers)	
England and Wales	129,026
Scotland	14,810
Northern Ireland	12,464
Total	**156,300**

Source: George and Button (2000: 30); parliamentary questions.
Notes:
1. Security officers include cash-in-transit officers.
2. Police numbers relate to 1999; Northern Ireland statistics include full and part-time reserve officers.

The growth in the numbers of large spaces open to the public but privately owned (shopping centres, for example) has been another factor, as these spaces are primarily policed by private security firms. The government and private companies promote the use of security products and services in attempts to deter crime. Finally, as more and more houses and factories are built, the more new security products and services are required.

Private security and policing

The private security industry supplies policing functions in terms of both personnel and products (George and Button 2000). Many of the products it supplies need human assistance to operate effectively, although there is now a growing number of complex systems that require little or no input from human beings (e.g. speed cameras). While the focus of this chapter is on the personnel who work in the private security industry, there is, nevertheless, a growing body of literature on various security products – particularly CCTV – there is no space to consider here (Beck and Willis 1995; Gill 1994, 1998; Norris et al 1998; George and Button 2000).

The 1993 white paper on police reform identified four broad aims for the police: to fight and prevent crime; to uphold the law; to bring to justice those who break the law; and to protect, help and reassure the community. All these roles are pursued in varying degrees by the private sector. Almost all private security measures are targeted at preventing crime. They are also used to uphold not only the internal rules of the organisations where they operate but also the law. Although bringing to justice those who break the law could hardly be described as one of the main functions of private security, there is a significant element of this. In the retail sector, for example, security personnel are involved each year in around one million cases of apprehending customers and staff for theft, which are handed over to the police for prosecution (British Retail Consortium 1999). Much of the equipment used by the private security industry is also vital in bringing offenders to justice (e.g. video evidence from CCTV cameras). Finally, the private security industry is involved in protecting, helping and reassuring those who pay for its services. This role often overlaps with that of protecting employees at work, the public in private places and the public when it has purchased private security services.

Perhaps, therefore, the only thing the public police in the UK still have a monopoly on is the use of firearms. This is not, however, the case in many other countries, where private security personnel are often routinely armed (De Waard 1993). The General Orders of the Fort Worth Police Department (USA) outline the range of force officers should employ and the conditions for when they should employ it (cited in McKenzie and Gallagher 1989). Level 1 force is officer presence; level 2 verbal commands; level 3 control and restrain; and level 3a control and restrain (a slight increase). These types of force are all frequently used by certain types of security personnel. Door supervisors (bouncers), for example, often have to use these levels of force in the course of the duties when the use of such force is legal and, unfortunately, all too often when it is not. Security officers working in shopping centres and courts may also use this range of force. Level 4 (chemical agents) is not a legal option in the UK for private security personnel, nor is level 5 (temporary in-capacitation) – although there have been calls for security officers to be armed with truncheons and vapour sprays by some influential people (the Chairman of Dixons, Sir Stanley Kalms, cited in *Security Gazette* October 1997). One suspects, however, there may be a significant number of security personnel who carry such weapons illegally for their own protection. Finally, level 6 (deadly force) – although not frequently used by security personnel – has been used legally in some instances for self-defence and also illegally. An unpublished Association of Chief Police Officers' report on door supervisors illustrated how people had been assaulted, seriously injured or even killed by such supervisors (cited in British Entertainment and Discotheque Association 1995).

Jones and Newburn (1998) found that the Metropolitan Police Service (MPS) and the private security industry undertook the same tasks. Virtually every activity undertaken by the police was offered as a service by the private sector in some form or other. This is illustrated in table 8.2

While most private security personnel do not have any special statutory powers, they are still seen as figures of authority by the general public (Home Office 1979). As Sarre and Prenzler (1999: 24) have argued:

> Private security personnel are a formidable force for good or ill in modern society. In many countries they substantially outnumber the police. As agents of property owners they possess considerable powers, and their authority, while on private property, more often than not exceeds that of conventional police. It is therefore somewhat anomalous that questions regarding public police accountability continue to receive far more attention from academics, civil libertarians and policy makers than private operations do.

However, in undertaking their duties on private property as the agents of the property's owner, private security personnel have certain rights that can become de facto powers (Stenning and Shearing 1979a; Sarre 1994). Depending upon the circumstances these powers include the right to search, the right to eject someone from the property and the right to interrogate. Other powers and privileges also apply when operating on private property, such as the ability to conduct intrusive surveillance (see below). Many security personnel similarly routinely use their citizen's right of arrest most of us would not consider using no matter how clearly the arrest would be classified as lawful. The extent of the use of some of these powers is illustrated in the annual British Retail Consortium Crime Costs survey. This survey contains statistics on the numbers of customers and staff apprehended for theft, as well as the numbers handed over to the police for prosecution. In 1998, 789,000 customers were apprehended by staff working for retailers (the vast majority being security staff), of whom 476,000 were referred to the police. Some 14,000 staff were also apprehended, of whom 7,000 were handed over to the police (British Retail Consortium 1999).

Table 8.2 Functional boundaries in policing

Function	Metropolitan Police	Parks Police	British Transport Police	Environmental health officers / Health and Safety Executive Inspectors	Housing patrol	Post Office Investigation Department	Private security
Respond to calls	✓	✓	✓		✓		✓
Investigate crime	✓	✓	✓	✓		✓	✓
Arrest offenders	✓	✓	✓			✓	✓
Maintain public order	✓	✓	✓				✓
Visible patrol	✓	✓	✓		✓		✓
Traffic control	✓	✓	✓		✓		✓
Parking enforcement	✓	✓	✓		✓		✓
Accident investigation	✓	✓	✓	✓			✓
Crime pattern analysis	✓	✓	✓			✓	✓
Security surveys	✓	✓	✓				✓
Alarm response	✓	✓			✓		✓
Noise/harassment	✓	✓		✓	✓		✓
Prisoner escort	✓						✓
CCTV monitoring	✓	✓	✓		✓		✓

Source: Jones and Newburn (1998).

The claim that private security personnel have no special powers would thus appear to be very misleading. As we have just seen, in the retail sector alone significant numbers of customers and staff have experienced the powers of security staff. Some private security personnel do, in fact, possess special statutory powers. Prison custody officers working in private prisons and prisoner escorts, for example, possess powers comparable to prison officers under the Criminal Justice Act 1991 and Criminal Justice and Public Order Act 1994. Security officers working in magistrates courts possess special powers of search and ejection set out in the Criminal Justice Act 1991. Generally, however, as we have seen, most private security officers do not possess such powers.

During the passage of the Police Act 1997 there was intense controversy over plans to allow chief police officers the power to authorise various types of intrusive surveillance. There have, however, been relatively few concerns expressed about the ability of public and private organisations to undertake intrusive surveillance on their own private space. There is a grey area here about the legality of employers tapping their own telephones and planting surveillance devices (such as covert CCTV cameras) on their own property. This has been illustrated recently by a number of high-profile cases. It was revealed recently in the press, for example, that Mohamed Al Fayed, the owner of Harrods, had ordered employees' private telephone calls to be monitored – not only for evidence of fraud but also for anything of a sexual nature, as well as for evidence of trade union activity (*The Observer* 30 November 1997). Shortly before this, however, the former Assistant Chief Constable of Merseyside, Alison Halford, had succeeded in the European Court of Human Rights in having the tapping of her private telephone calls on her work telephone declared an invasion of her privacy. Even after this judgment some experts were still advising that, as long as an appropriate clause exists in an employee's contract of employment stating that such surveillance may take place, such telephone tapping is lawful.

In the case of private investigators (and this includes private citizens), planting bugs that use an unauthorised radio transmitter or receiver and tapping private telephones are considered illegal activities (Cornwall 1991), even thought the punishment for such crimes is often minimal. For example, when private detective agency owner, Michael Anderson (who was also a former police officer) was convicted of the unlawful interception of communications in an industrial espionage case, his sentence was a mere 12 months' imprisonment, 9 months suspended (*The Times* 12 February 1988). These bugs and many other forms of surveillance equipment are, however, freely available in the UK. The Regulation of

Investigatory Powers Act 2000 and the Human Rights Act 1998, however, may lead to greater regulation in this area.

Most of the sophisticated surveillance equipment the police use is available for private security organisations (and ordinary citizens) to purchase. Any visit to a security exhibition or to a specialist shop will reveal the wide array of highly sophisticated equipment that can be used for surveillance purposes. There are, for instance, covert cameras that can be fitted in clocks and even sun-glasses. Various bugging devices are sold that, if used, would be illegal but that are still purchased in very large numbers in the UK (Davies 1996). Telephone-tapping devices can be bought, as can satellite-tracking devices. Even the spy satellites used during the 'Cold War' can be hired by private individuals to home in on objects as little as 3 metres in size – and for as little as £100 (*Security Gazette* November 1997).

Security officers and private investigators have also created their own intelligence-gathering networks. Liberty (1995) has provided evidence of security firms gathering intelligence about protesters at road-protest demonstrations. This involved photographing and following the protesters and there were also allegations of telephone tapping. Security staff in retailing gather intelligence on shop-lifters and share this knowledge with other security firms and the police. Security staff employed in such places as abattoirs have been known to gather intelligence on animal rights protesters. Indeed, McDonald's was found recently to have used private investigators to infiltrate a group of London environmentalists which, it believed, had libelled the company (Vidal 1997).

Public order policing

Two important examples illustrate the growing role private security plays in public order policing. The first is the policing of the night-time economy (NTE), which is largely undertaken by door supervisors (Hobbs, Lister *et al* 2000). The second is the policing of protests, particularly environmental protests (Button *et al* 2001).

Door supervisors (bouncers) are considered by many to have become the primary force policing the NTE (Lister *et al* 2000). In town and city centres at night, while there will only be a handful of police officers on duty, there will be dozens if not hundreds of door supervisors outside pubs, clubs and takeaways, etc. These people are employed to control access to the premises and to ensure order is maintained in the areas they protect (Walker 1999). Much of the violence that takes place in society now occurs in and around licensed premises during the NTE. For instance, in one study it was found that 45 per cent of all logs for violence were made between the hours of 21.00 and 03.00 (Hobbs, Lister *et al* 2000). Door supervisors, therefore, have a significant role to play in ensuring public safety in such places. Many of the confrontations that take place are resolved without recourse to the police. In some venues there may be several thousand clients, and so door supervisors have major crowd-safety responsibilities.

To do their work, door supervisors employ a wide range of strategies. Many rely simply on their physical appearance. Physically large, 'hard' individuals may be able to carry out their duties without recourse to verbal or physical strategies. Some, however, must rely on their verbal skills to negotiate the end of a conflict (not always successfully), and they frequently have to resort to some form of violence, which is not always lawful. Indeed, some door supervisors resort to physical violence not as a means of protection but as a means of punishment. As Hobbs, Hall *et al* (2000) write: 'The acceptance amongst denizens of the night-time economy of levels of violence unparalleled outside military and penal institutions is astounding. It became obvious to us that very few of the violent incidents that occur are ever brought to the attention of the health or police authorities.'

There is in fact a great deal of evidence that illustrates the violence meted out by door supervisors. In the British Entertainment and Discotheque Association (BEDA) submission to the 1995 Home Affairs Committee inquiry into the private security industry, an Association of Chief Police Officers' report on door supervisors was cited that gives numerous examples of customers who have been seriously injured or killed in different constabulary areas (British Entertainment and Discotheque Association 1995). It would seem fair to suggest that far more people are assaulted, seriously injured and killed by door supervisors than police officers every year, yet these incidents receive relatively little attention compared to those involving the police. Concerns have been expressed over door supervisors operating protection rackets, dealing in drugs and of not being of suitable character (British Entertainment and Discotheque Association 1995; Walker 1999; Hobbs, Hall *et al* 2000). Indeed, a survey of 476 door supervisors in Liverpool identified 3 with murder/manslaughter convictions, 2 on bail charged with murder, 25 with weapons convictions, 7 with firearms convictions, 18 with drugs convictions, 101 with assault convictions and 97 claiming unemployment benefit while working regularly as door supervisors (British Entertainment and Discotheque Association 1995). Given these problems, it is not surprising that some localities have initiated schemes to register, vet and train door supervisors (some of which have met with only limited success). These schemes are explored in greater depth in Chapter 10.

The policing of environmental protests is another important area that has witnessed a growth in private sector involvement in recent years. Many of these protests have taken place on private space property, which has led to legal challenges to the right of protesters to occupy private land. The tactics the protesters used led many organisations to seek the protection only the private sector can supply. As a consequence, organisations have had to make use of substantial numbers of private security officers, particularly when evicting protesters (Button *et al* 2001). At the height of the Newbury protests, for example, over 1,000 security officers were involved (Vidal 1996a).

Private security officers are frequently employed before, during and after the eviction process (Button and John forthcoming). Their primary role is to protect the property from acts of sabotage, from theft and from further occupation. This usually entails standing guard at vulnerable locations, patrolling the property and keeping the property under surveillance. During the eviction process, security officers usually form a cordon around areas where evictions or construction work are taking place to prevent further intrusions of protesters. Needless to say, this tactic often involves physical confrontation with the protesters.

There have been many criticisms of the tactics used by some of the security officers at these protests. Given that some of these officers have received no (or only two days) training, this does not seem surprising. Police officers, who undergo extensive public order training and who attend control and restraint courses, often make mistakes. Perhaps of more concern has been the alleged attitude of some managers at these protests. Vidal managed to secure work as a security officer at Newbury. There he heard one manager at a briefing say: 'Anything in the trees today you whack it, right? Thwack it with your helmet. Anything. And don't get caught' (Vidal 1996b: 2). He also found that numerous security officers were eager to become involved in violence with the protesters. For instance, one officer explained to him: 'I'm here for the action. It's like a hunt, in'it? You take out someone and you know you've got two men backing you up' (ibid.: 3).

These examples of door supervisors and security officers at environmental protests raise a number of issues, such as their suitability for many of the roles they are expected to play, the value of the training they receive and their accountability. There has been a long debate in academic and political circles about these issues (South 1988; Jones and Newburn 1998; George and Button 2000). Given the nature of this work, there should be restrictions on the types of characters who are employed to undertake this work. Similarly, there should be statutory minimum standards of training. Some of these issues are explored in more detail in Chapter 10.

Investigative policing

Unlike the popular image, private investigators rarely investigate such serious crimes as murder. They may, however, be employed by clients to investigate such a crime when the police consider there is insufficient evidence of a crime having been committed in an attempt to regain the police's interest (Gill and Hart 1997a). They may also be used by the defence in a criminal trial to secure evidence that could lead to an acquittal. Investigators in the private sector, however, are largely involved in the investigation of deviant behaviour, where criminal prosecution is not the ultimate aim.

There is a large number of specialist, high-quality private investigator firms (such as Carratu, Control Risks and Kroll) whose main purpose is to investigate large-scale frauds (Gill and Hart 1997b). Many organisations have have been subjected to fraud do not want the bad publicity a police investigation might bring, preferring to try to get their money back rather than prosecute the offender (Gill and Hart 1997a). Not all investigations involve large-scale fraud. For example, a Manchester City Council worker who was making a claim for £100,000 for a shoulder injury was put under surveillance by the council through a firm of private investigators. The surveillance found him lifting luggage, swimming and even hauling himself from the swimming pool. After seeing the footage with his trade union representative, this worker was advised to withdraw his claim (Spencer 1994). Many false claims are investigated like this, and the aim is not to prosecute but to prevent loss or recover monies lost. There are other areas where the police have limited expertise (or little interest) in conducting investigations. Industrial espionage, counterfeiting and product tampering are all areas where private investigators are used and where criminal prosecution is not the aim (Gregory 1994; George and Button 2000).

Private investigators might even become involved in hostage negotiations. When three telecommunications engineers were kidnapped while working in Chechya, negotiations took place between investigators from Control Risks and the kidnappers. Unfortunately these negotiations failed, and the three engineers were executed (Buncombe *et al* 1998). Investigators similarly become involved in due diligence inquiries – companies that are for sale are investigated to determine if the value they are claiming is accurate (Gill and Hart 1997a). Private investigators are also used in intelligence gathering for a wide range of causes (Murray 1993; Vidal 1997; Button 1998). These are just some of the many activities private investigators become involved in when engaged in criminal investigations. They are, however, also used in many non-criminal investigations, such as those concerning personal relationships, the characters of prospective employees and tracing missing persons.

In undertaking these investigation they use many of the tactics the police use – and more. Because the aim of the investigation is not usually criminal prosecution or civil litigation, these investigators are not bound by the regulations the police face. It should also be remembered that many private investigators are ex-police detectives and therefore have substantial investigatory skills and contacts. One of the tactics they use in information gathering is to conduct interviews, often employing persuasion or trickery or putting the interviewee under pressure through the use of their employment contracts. Searches are also done using similar tactics. Many investigators have access to a wide range of sophisticated databases, which can be used to secure information about addresses, financial circumstances and affiliations to organisations, etc. Investigators may also use 'pretext' inquiries to secure information where they pretend to be someone they are not (for instance, telephoning someone claiming to be a market researcher). Information may also be obtained by sifting through a target's rubbish. Finally, information may be gained illegally from contacts in the public security services. Private investigators also engage in surveillance, using observation teams as would the police. As discussed above, they also have access to virtually all the technology the police have access to, such as covert CCTV, listening devices, tracking systems, etc.

Police–private security co-operation

Given the increasing role of the private security industry in policing, it would be of interest to know the extent of its relationship with the police. Unfortunately in the UK there is virtually no research that explores this relationship. In Canada, however, there is research that suggests the police are often quite negative about private security (Shearing *et al* 1985; Stenning 1989). Given the negative image private security has amongst the public in general, this is not surprising (Livingstone and Hart forthcoming). In recent years in the UK, however, there have been signs the police are beginning to realise the benefits of working actively with the private security industry (see Blair's ideas in Chapter 9). This more positive relationship could be seen as a move towards stage five (active partnership), in Stenning's (1989) model of police–private security co-operation. Stenning's model of police–private security co-operation is as follows.

1 *Denial.* Police officers refuse to acknowledge private security officers are a legitimate topic of discussion.
2 *Grudging recognition.* Grudging recognition is accompanied by denigration. The increased role private security plays can no longer be ignored but there is a belief private security officers are undertaking lesser activities, such as property protection.
3 *Competition and open hostility.* The relationship moves to one of competition and open hostility. The growth of private security poses a threat to the police's claimed monopoly over policing. At the same time, private security is recognised as a source of employment on retirement and as a means to provide policing services under stretched budgets.
4 *Calls for greater controls.* There are calls for greater controls on the industry, which is now viewed as either a necessary evil or as a legitimate component of policing.
5 *Active partnership.* Active partnership arises when it is realised private security has a significant role to play in policing.
6 *Equal partnership.* Finally Stenning identified a stage that had not yet been reached in Canada at the time he was writing, that of equal partnership between the police and private security.

The state of relations between the police and private security in the UK has probably now reached stages four and five. Most police officers now recognise the contribution private security can make to policing, and the main concern now is for greater regulation and control. Few, however, would call for an active partnership. Blair's speech on 'police-compliant' security officers (discussed in the next chapter) perhaps represents the first occasion when a senior British police officer recognised the benefits of active partnership. It seems inevitable, therefore, that more officers will now begin to recognise the benefits of active partnership. To what extent the partnership will ever reach one of equals, however, is difficult to assess: there seems at the moment to be very few (if any) examples of where private security officers are treated as equals to the police.

Chapter 9

'Plural policing': the patrol

While the previous chapter outlined in general the growing role the private security industry plays in policing, this chapter examines in more detail the police's patrolling function as this is one of the best examples of the 'pluralisation' or 'fragmentation' of policing. Patrolling has been the topic of recent heated debates about the roles and activities the police, private security firms and other agencies fulfil. It is also one of the most overt activities the public police undertake. As the Audit Commission (1996: 5) has argued: 'It [patrol] provides a sense of security and symbolises lawful authority at a time when there are increasing concerns about an erosion of authority.'

The importance of police patrols

Street patrols by uniformed police officers is still regarded as one of the police's most important functions. In a poll conducted for the Police Federation in 1995, 80 per cent of respondents wanted more police patrolling their neighbourhoods. The same research found that only one person in a hundred wanted less patrolling. Research conducted for the Audit Commission in 1996 similarly found there was significant public dissatisfaction at the level of foot patrols. The same research also found that 72 per cent of people are reassured by the sight of a patrol officer when they are feeling vulnerable for some reason. While there thus seems to be an insatiable desire for uniformed police officers on the streets, a great deal of research has demonstrated the ineffectiveness of police patrols as a method of crime prevention and detection. Indeed some research has shown that a constable on patrol is likely to pass within 100 yards of a burglary every 8 years (Police Foundation/Policy Studies Institute 1996).

In a now famous experiment conducted in Kansas City, Kelling *et al* (1974) found that increasing the level of mobile patrol by as much as two or three times had no discernible effect on the level of crime. Studies in Newark, New Jersey, and Flint, Michigan, showed similar results (Police Foundation/Policy Studies Institute 1996). In an overview of the literature about police patrols, Loveday (1998) highlighted the low status this policing function is given. There is, however, some research that demonstrates benefits of police patrols. As noted earlier, the sight of police officers on patrol reassures the public and reduces the fear of crime (Audit Commission 1996). There is also evidence that patrols in areas where crime is rife can reduce the level of crime (Sherman 1990). Finally, while there is mixed evidence about the effectiveness of so-called 'zero tolerance' policing strategies (Hopkins-Burke 1998), the evidence demonstrates that a uniformed police presence on the streets has little effect on crime rates.

Police managers, therefore, are faced with the dilemma of satisfying the publics demand for 'bobbies on the beat' while, at the same time, using their resources in the most efficient manner possible to prevent and tackle crime. In a typical force of 2,500 officers, only 125 individuals would normally be on patrol (the others would be on leave, sick, in courts, etc.). Putting more bobbies on the beat, therefore, is a difficult task (Audit Commission 1996). Police officers are also very expensive to employ. In 1996, for example, it was estimated that a police constable cost £32,000 per year, compared to £18,000 for a local authority patrol officer and £12,000 for a security officer (ibid.).

It would be wrong, however, to suggest that the police have a monopoly in patrolling the streets. As Table 9.1 illustrates, a wide range of different policing bodies patrol public areas, and many of these organisations have a long history of doing so. What is new, however, is the increasing use of non-police personnel to patrol public streets. This is not, perhaps, surprising given the public's desire to see more 'bobbies on the beat'. An example of a non-police patrolling body is Sedgefield Borough Community Force (I'Anson and Wiles, undated). This local authority policing body began its operations in January 1994, providing a 24-hour patrolling service to over 90,000 people. Its officers wear uniforms similar to those of the public police, but they have no special powers. Some of their roles include consulting residents about anti-social problems, liaising with the police about crime trends, providing advice to the community about crime prevention and gathering evidence about

Table 9.1 Uniformed personnel who patrol public areas

The public police
Special constables
Special police forces
Traffic wardens
Caretakers
Local authority wardens
Volunteers
   Supported by the police
   Discouraged by thepolice
Private security officers
   In private spaces open to public
   In public spaces

anti-social behaviour. In 1998 the force received 1,877 requests for action, 103 alarm calls and 67,921 radio calls. It also had 708 contacts of various kinds with the police. It has been estimated that crime fell by 20 per cent in the first year of its operation, according to police figures (although it might be wrong to attribute all this to this force). Research found that 93 per cent of customers considered the promptness of the service 'excellent' or 'good' and that 95 per cent considered the officers 'very helpful' or 'helpful' (Jacobsen and Saville 1999).

A similar force operates in Southwark, south London, on the Aylesbury estate, where the local authority employs a private security firm to patrol the streets. This scheme was created to combat the fear of crime, anti-social behaviour, graffiti and drug abuses etc. It is managed by the Taplow neighbourhood office and is put out to tender each year (Jacobsen and Saville 1999). The Stockport Town Wardens is another example of a contracted-out patrolling force. This is funded by a £100,000 grant from the Single Regeneration Budget (SRB). These wardens play a similar role to the Sedgefield officers and are recruited from the ranks of the unemployed on one-year contracts (Jenkins 1998).

A number of patrols have emerged in residential areas, operated by private security companies and funded by subscriptions from local residents. These patrols have received 'lukewarm' support from the police and, in some cases, even hostility. For example, Household Security of Doncaster (founded by an ex-offender, Malcolm Tetley) provides uniformed patrols for a weekly fee of £1 per household. In 1996 it was estimated this company had 3,000 customers (Sharp and Wilson 2000). Customers are given a window sticker that says 'Warning: these premises patrolled by Household Security'. Sharp and Wilson found that most customers were satisfied with Household Security's more pro-activce attitude to problems compared to the attitude of the police. They also found there was a belief the company would use informal methods, (such as a 'kick up the backside') in comparison to the police, and that this was considered to be more effective. The local police were very lukewarm towards the whole venture in their public pronouncements, and Tetley believed the police were harassing his staff and 'rubbing' them in public.

Noaks (2000) investigated an 'entrepreneurial' private patrol scheme in the anonymous estate of 'Merryside'. As with the Doncaster example, this private security firm (consisting of a managing director and five guards) provides a patrolling service to an estate of 4,000 homes for a fee of £2 per household per week (pensioners paid £1). Noaks found a high degree of satisfaction amongst the subscribers, with 92 per cent either satisfied or very satisfied with the service and over three-quarters considering crime had declined in the area as a result of the patrol. Of the non-subscribers, only 25 per cent were dissatisfied with the service. As with Doncaster schemes, there was a degree of hostility towards the company from the local police, such that it was excluded from a local partnership under the Crime and Disorder Act 1998. These examples illustrate the generally positive regard residents have for these types of initiatives, as confirmed by McManus (1995), as well as the negative response the police have shown towards such 'entrepreneurial' initiatives.

Estimates of the numbers of such organised patrols are difficult to find, but one article published in 1993 put them at over 1,000 (although this was based upon no hard evidence) (Birch 1993). Research conducted for the government's Neighbourhood Wardens initiative was able to collate information gathered from 50 such (Jacobson and Saville 1999). Whatever the level of this kind of patrol it seems certain they are growing in numbers as a result of the government's encouragement of Neighbourhood Wardens and through changing police attitudes.

International perspectives

In response to a growing demand for more police on the streets, a new police rank has been created in the rank of police constable in The Netherlands. Below the rank of police constable, the *Politiesurveillant* or police patroller rank has been established. These officers wear full police uniform, hold police powers and are eligible to become constables after a satisfactory period of service. Another scheme developed in The

Netherlands is the 'city warden' or *Stadswacht*. These wardens, often drawn from the unemployed, provide a visible daytime police presence on city streets. While they possess no special powers, they are seen as the police's 'eyes and ears' (Police Foundation/Policy Studies Institute 1996). A number of experiments along these lines have also been conducted in the USA. Starrett City Corporation employs its own private police force comprising officers who hold police powers. Research has shown this force has contributed to a lowering of the crime rate, when compared to similar neighbourhoods. This has been achieved through a merger of community interest, community need and an appropriate policing style (Shearing 1996). In Philadelphia, the Security Watch Program similarly utilises police-trained security officers as the eyes and ears of the police department. (ibid.).

Squaring the circle of an increasing uniformed presence on the streets

Given the importance to the public of a uniformed presence on the streets, it is not surprising to find that a wide range of proposals has been put forward to try to solve this problem, emanating from think- tanks, police officers and government bodies. For example, the 1996 Audit Commission report on police patrols made a wide range of recommendations, the most significant of which were reforms to the shift system and the payment of retainers for special constables. The Police Foundation (PF) and Policy Studies Institute (PSI) in their inquiry *The Roles and the Responsibilities of the Police* (1996), put forward four, more radical, alternatives:

1 The establishment of local authority patrols as the 'eyes and ears' of the police along the lines of the Sedgefield Community Force.
2 The establishment of local authority patrols as the 'eyes and ears' of the police but contracted out to private security companies.
3 The establishment of municipal police forces comprising officers with special powers similar to those of the Wandsworth Parks Constabulary.
4 Greater experimentation in the police service, with the new ranks below that of constable dedicated solely to patrolling.

More recently, the former Chief Constable of Surrey, Ian Blair, has advocated the deployment of 'police compliant' security officers. Under this scheme, licensed security officers would wear badges that said 'police compliant' and would carry police radios, but they would have no special powers. These officers would be an auxiliary of the police service. Opponents of Blair's proposals have expressed the fear that the police would lose their monopoly over public patrol. In reality, however, the police have not had this monopoly for some time, if ever (see Johnston 1992a). As Blair (1998: 4) has argued: '… it is not abandoning a monopoly of patrol – it is admitting we haven't had one for years and then moving the discussion on.'

Blair has thus proposed a new patrolling force (under *police* control) that would be employed by local authorities, private security companies or the police themselves. In terms of Stenning's (1989) model discussed in Chapter 8, the UK has perhaps reached the stage of 'active partnership'.

The New Labour government – through its Social Exclusion Unit (SEU) – has also put forward a range of policy initiatives in this area. One of these (emanating from research into Neighbourhood Wardens) resulted in a report that advocated an extension of their use (Policy Action Team 6 2000). Neighbourhood wardens usually operate in one particular area where they are involved in a range of activities: including patrolling; environmental improvements (such as repairing properties); and community development (such as organising community events) (Jacobsen and Saville 1999). The report was followed by an announcement that £18.5 million was to be made available until 2003–2004 to fund such schemes, 86 schemes having already been funded (Home Office 2001). The criminal justice plan published by the Home Office (2001) has also endorsed Blair's ideas and contains plans for the promotion and evaluation of such schemes.

At the time of writing (October 2001) MPS plans were also leaked to the media to establish a new force of 800 civilian patrol officers. These would effectively be officers of sub-constable level employed to undertake uniformed patrols, investigate minor crimes, issue fixed penalty notices for traffic offences amongst other functions. They would be paid £17,500 per annum, which is about £8,500 less than a constable, and trained to a lesser standard. They would possess limited special powers to detain suspects, stop vehicles and confiscate drugs, but they would not possess the full powers of a constable. The proposals are also expected to be adopted by other forces nationwide and have the support of the Home Office. Not surprisingly the plans drew criticism from the Police Federation of 'policing on the cheap' and a 'confidence trick' (Bennetto 2001). It also seems inevitable that once established many of these officers will increasingly demand increasing parity with their fellow constables on their powers, protection (CS gas, vests etc.) and most likely pay and conditions. Given the public's insatiable desire for a uniformed presence on the streets, however, they represent an innovative way to square the circle of increasing uniformed presence on the streets, that carries adequate authority that is cost effective. The proposals also illustrate the sequential development of Blair's original ideas of police accredited security patrols, to a more sophisticated mix of plural policing provision.

The prospect of more plural policing

The main benefit of more plural policing for patrols would be the ability to satisfy the public's demand for an increased uniformed presence on the streets. As such officers would require fewer skills and less training than the traditional police, they would not have to be paid as much as traditional police officers. Indeed, the Audit Commission estimated that the cost of an 'auxiliary patrol officer' would be £25,000 per annum, compared to £32,000 for a constable. It might even be possible to reduce this even further, given the comparatively low pay most private security officers receive. Set against this, however, is the effectiveness of such officers. While researching the public's attitudes to various occupations, the Audit Commission found that on a scale of plus 100 to minus 100 a police officer on foot reassured the public by more than plus 80 per cent, whereas security officers provided assurance of minus 20 per cent and traffic wardens minus 60 per cent (Audit Commission 1996). Dedicated street patrol officers would probably be a cross between the two. Thus while there might be more officers on the beat, their net contribution to levels of public safety would be less than the alternative of putting a lesser number of constables on the beat.

Officers dedicated to patrolling the streets would free up the remaining police officers to become involved in more complex crime-reduction strategies. Set against this, however, would be the concern that the same numbers of constables were being employed. In fact, when prisoner escorting was contracted out to the private sector, one of the aims was to free more officers for the beat. The result, however, was a reduction in officer numbers. In the MPS area, for example, 271 officers were lost between October 1994 and March 1995 (*Hansard* 3 November 1994). Another concern would be that the police had become agents of crime control and enforcement, dealing less often with the public in non-crime-orientated situations. This could change the nature of the public police and the way the public perceive them.

Another advantage of dedicated patrol officers is that they would have an expertise in patrolling. The Officers could be trained specifically for this role. Also, because they would be most likely to patrol one particular area, they would develop an extensive knowledge of that area and could hence, target their patrolling more effectively.

It could be argued this has already happened as a result of privately funded police patrols. If a new patrol function were to be created that addressed the public's demand for patrols, this might go some way to reducing the necessity for such schemes. One of the main disadvantages of a new patrolling force would be the possibility the public might not have confidence in them. As noted above, research has illustrated that the public have negative perceptions of private security guards and traffic wardens (Audit Commission 1996). As patrol officers would likely be a 'hybrid' of these, it might be reasonable to assume they, too, would generate a similarly low level of reassurance. Also as they would be recruited from a lower end of the labour market and trained to a lesser extent than police constables they might be less capable of dealing with situations police constables deal with routinely. If this happened frequently this might reduce further the public's expectations of them. McManus (1995) – in his research into private security patrols – found, however, over time, the public's confidence in such patrols began to grow.

Chapter 10

The regulation of private policing

The previous chapters have illustrated the extensive roles of the wide range of public, private, hybrid and municipal organisations that are engaged in policing, particularly the growing role of the private security industry, while there are concerns about the accountability and control of many of these bodies, most anxieties concern the private security industry. As Stenning and Shearing (1979b: 263) have argued: 'If private security personnel are in reality no different from ordinary citizens, a law which treats them alike seems most appropriate. But if in reality they are not, and the law still treats them as they are, it becomes inappropriate.'

The previous chapters have also shown that private security personnel are in fact not like ordinary citizens as they do things most citizens would rarely consider doing. The aim of this chapter is, therefore, to examine the current – largely voluntary – structures that regulate the British private security industry. Some of the international experience of regulation is then explored, using George and Button's (1997) model of analysis. The chapter then moves on to outline briefly some of the provisions of the Private Security Industry Act 2001. Finally, it examines more radical ideas for regulating policing as identified by Loader (2000).

The regulatory structure of the British private security industry

According to Francis (1993: 5) regulation can be defined as: '... state intervention in private spheres of activity to realise public purposes.' The private security industry is subject to a great deal of regulation relating to company law, employment law and health and safety legislation, etc.

Even in the area of licensing there are already statutory regulations governing private security industry (Button and George 2001). Aviation and maritime security, atomic energy security, private prisons and escorts and guard dogs are also areas already subject to government regulation. However, until the implementation of the Private Security Industry Act 2001 (which is discussed later), most of the regulation governing the industry is voluntary. Those regulations that apply to state guarding, private investigation and door supervision are considered here; those sectors of the private security industry that are less directly engaged in policing are not considered (those interested are referred to George and Button 2000).

The static, manned guarding sector

The regulation of the static, manned guarding sector relies upon a firm's membership of trade associations and/or inspectorates. The two trade associations are the British Security Industry Association (BSIA) and the International Professional Security Association (IPSA). Companies that are members of the BSIA must also register with the National Security Inspectorate (NSI) or another independent certification body accredited by the United Kingdom Accreditation Service (UKAS). The NSI uses as standards for this sector British Standards (BS) 7499 (the code of practice for static guarding, mobile patrol and keyholding services); BS 7858 (the code of practice for the security screening of personnel); and BS European Norm (EN) International Standards Organisation (ISO) 9000 (the international quality assurance standard). Various categories of registration are based upon these standards. The NSI is also approved by UKAS as an independent certification body. The NSI was created in 2001 from the merger of the Inspectorate of the Security Industry (ISI) and the National Approval Council for Security Systems (NACOSS).

This regulation is purely voluntary, and out of an estimated 1,000 plus companies, only some 250 are members of one of these associations or inspectorates. Nevertheless, these companies probably account for nearly three-quarters of the personnel working in this sector. The regulations do not cover individual security employees, only the firms. There have been criticisms that these standards are kept to the minimum in order to maximise membership of these bodies (George and Button 1996). If a firm is disciplined it may elect to resign from the association or inspectorate in order to avoid paying the penalty.

Private investigators

Regulation of the private investigation sector is slightly different as it is based upon individual rather than organisational membership. It is, however, self-regulating and voluntary. The two main associations are the Association of British Investigators (ABI) and the Institute of Professional Investigators (IPI). To join these associations, investigators must be able to meet basic entrance requirements, which are based upon character and professional knowledge. The requirements of the IPI are, however, more academic. Both associations have codes of ethics members must adhere to, and breaches of these codes can result in disciplinary action. Some private investigators are also certificated bailiffs, which requires them to meet certain standards of character and to be approved by a judge. Some investigators use this status to prove they are of reputable character (Button 1998). In this sector, therefore, there are no British Standards, no independent inspectorates and no regulatory structures for firms. It has been estimated there are around 500 members of these two associations (some join both) out of an estimated 15,000 private investigators (ibid.). The same criticisms concerning interest and disciplinary sanctions discussed earlier also apply to this sector.

Door supervisors

The regulation of the door supervision sector is different again (although BS 7960 has emerged in recent years as a standard for door supervisors). The self-regularory structure that does exist applies only to individuals (and only to a tiny proportion of all door supervisors operating in this sector). Given this lack of standards it is not surprising many local regulatory schemes have been created. These schemes attached conditions to a pub or night-club's public entertainment licence that their door supervisors must be registered with a specific body (Walker 1999). Registration means the door supervisors must come up to minimum character requirements and must undertake a course of training. They must also abide by a code of practice (although schemes vary in this). It is estimated that only around a half of local authorities have such schemes, although most large towns and cities do have them (Hobbs, Lister *et al* 2000). Some schemes are compulsory while others are voluntary, and some have minimum training standards. Research conducted by Hobbs, Hall *et al* (2000) identified a number of problems with these schemes. These included the requirement for door supervisors to register with different local authorities, thus duplicating their training and vetting, at great expense to the door supervisors. It was also found that standards varied significantly between schemes, such that some door supervisors could be granted registration in one area but not in another. The enforcement of the schemes was also often found to be chaotic, and revocation of a door supervisor's registration was a rare event. For instance, in one scheme assessed by Hobbs, Hall *et al* (ibid.), not one licence had been revoked in 3½ years despite over 42 alleged assaults by door supervisors. Finally, these researchers found various systems in use to get around registration procedures.

Individual accountability: the missing link?

The most important gap in these voluntary structures is a lack of individual accountability. Given that many of these personnel undertake duties that could cause distress to the public and to their clients, their accountability is a legitimate concern. If someone is dissatisfied with a security officer's performance, what options are open to him or her? First, there are the disciplinary procedures of the organisation concerned. However, the officer may be a sole trader, may work for a small firm or the organisation may not give the complaint the attention it deserves. So if this first option fails, the complainant might consider the second option of civil litigation. However, this usually requires substantial funds. Thirdly, if the criminal law has been broken, the police could be called – something that frequently occurs with allegations of excessive violence by door supervisors. For this to be successful, however, there must be evidence, and this is not always available. Indeed, research on door supervisors has revealed there is a reluctance to report incidents of violence, a disinclination by the police to record and investigate such incidents and a 'code of silence' amongst door supervisors – all of which makes prosecutions difficult (Lister *et al* 2000). Finally, in the case of private investigators, if they are members of the ABI or IPI, a complaint could be made to these organisations. Even if disciplinary procedures were pursued, however, these organisations could not ban the investigator from practising and, if the penalty was too harsh, all the investigator would have to do would be to resign from the association.

International approaches to controlling the private security industry

In most industrialised countries, the state has responded to the growth of private security by creating some form of statutory framework within which the industry must operate (Shearing and Stenning 1981; George and Button 1997; De Waard 1999; Prenzler and Sarre 1999; Yoshida 1999). The countries that have created such frameworks include all the states in the European Union (except Greece and the Republic of Ireland, although legislation was introduced into the Republic of Ireland in early 2001); Hong Kong, Hungary, Jamaica, Japan, New Zealand, Russia and Trinidad and Tobago, to name but a few. In countries that have federal systems of government there is often regulation at state level. In the USA, for example, 42 states and Washington DC all have such a framework, as do all the provinces of Canada and all the states and territories of Australia (George and Button 1997; Prenzler and Sarre 1999). In some of these jurisdictions the regulations have been in place for a considerable length of time. The State of Missouri passed a statute regulating private detectives in 1885, Pennsylvania in 1887 and New York in 1898 (Moore 1990). In Ontario the licensing of private detectives can be traced back to 1909 (Slater 1982). In Europe, too, there has been a long tradition of regulating private investigators. Legislation was enacted in Italy in 1940, in France in 1942 and in Switzerland in 1943 (Button 1998). The nature of these regulatory systems, however, varies considerably between countries (George and Button 1997). The following section illustrates some of these differences.

Regulatory systems compared

George and Button (1997) have identified three broad characteristics of regulations that can be used to compare and contrast the myriad of systems in existence globally. These are the width of regulation, (how many sectors of the industry are regulated), the depth of regulation (the number and type of regulations to be met by security firms and their employees) and, finally, the agent responsible for regulation. Having identified these three characteristics of private security regulatory systems and having analysed the first two, George and Button (ibid.) were able to identify five models of regulation, which are set out in Table 10.1.

The Republic of Ireland and Great Britain (before the introduction of legislation in 2001) are examples of the non-interventionist model. Northern Ireland is an example of the minimum narrow model, where the only standard that applies is an investigation into the background/ character of contract guarding firms, plus a few other minor requirements. New Zealand is an example of the minimum wide model, where the contract manned guarding sector, private investigators and installers of certain security equipment are subject to regulation. These standards, however, mostly relate to character, and there are no minimum training standards. Denmark is an example of the comprehensive narrow model, where both the contract manned guarding sector and private

Table 10.1 Five models of regulation

Non-interventionist	There is no statutory licensing system for the private security industry (although there might be some special regulatory measures)
Minimum narrow	Minimal regulations apply (such as character requirements) but these only extend to the manned guarding and/or private investigator sectors
Minimum wide	Regulation applies to the wider private security industry but only with minimum requirements
Comprehensive narrow	There are regulations that seek to raise the quality of the industry (such as training standards for employees and standards of operation for firms) but these only apply to manned guarding and/or private investigators
Comprehensive wide	Quality-enhancing regulations are applied to the wider private security industry

investigations are regulated. However, in the case of contract manned guarding, comprehensive standards must be met by both employers and employees that go beyond mere character requirements to standards that are likely to increase the quality of private security. Security officers, for instance, must complete 120 hours of training within six months. Finally, Belgium is an example of the comprehensive wide model. This country regulates the manned guarding sector (including in-house), private investigators and alarm installers. This system includes standards intended to improve quality for both employers and employees. These standards include 120 hours' training (including an exam) as well as additional training for other specialist roles (a further 16 hours for guard-dog handlers, for instance). Table 10.2 shows how England and Wales compare to the rest of the European Union.

Having identified different models of regulation, George and Button attempted to identify 'best practice'. Despite the lack of reliable data enabling comparisons to be made, one writer has produced a performance table of European contract guarding sectors based upon wage levels, working hours, training of security officers, industrial relations, activities of professional associations, the size of the industry and the regulatory system (Berglund, undated). As the paper only applies

Table 10.2 England and Wales compared to the rest of the European Union

	Narrow	Wide
Minimal	Austria	
	France	
	Italy	
	Luxembourg	
	Northern Ireland	
	England and Wales	
Comprehensive	Denmark	Belgium
	Finland	The Netherlands
	Germany	Portugal
	Spain	*Republic of Ireland*
		Sweden

Note:
Italics indicates legislation is proposed or yet to be implemented.

to the contract guarding sector conclusions about the most effective type of regulatory system could only be applied to the 'depth' characteristic of George and Button's analysis.

The top five countries (Sweden, Belgium, The Netherlands, Norway and Denmark) all had 'comprehensive' regulatory systems. Of the top ten, eight had 'comprehensive' systems: the previous five plus Spain, Finland and Portugal, with France and Italy having 'Minimal' systems. The remaining eight countries in the table have either 'Minimal' systems or adopt a 'Non-Interventionist' approach: Luxembourg, Switzerland, Ireland, the UK, Austria, Germany, Greece and Hungary (Berglund was writing around 1995).

A caveat must be added, however, that there are several factors that contribute to the quality of private security provision. George and Button (1997) contend that one of these is the regulatory system in operation. Bearing this in mind and acknowledging the caveat just mentioned, they conclude that the 'comprehensive' system of regulation would seem to be the most effective in producing a higher-quality contract guarding sector.

Further evidence for identifying the most effective model of regulation can be obtained from reports on existing systems of regulations and statutes. In British Columbia, the Oppal Commission undertook an inquiry into the private security regulatory system and recommended the further widening and deepening of regulation (Oppal 1994). In the USA, a number of influential reports on the private security industry have identified models of regulation: the Department of Justice report of 1971 (Kakalik and Wildhorn 1971c) advocated what could be described as a 'comprehensive' model of regulation, and the 1976 report of the National Advisory Committee on Criminal Justice Standards and Goals advocated a 'comprehensive wide' model. The National Association of Security and Investigative Regulators has, in addition, drawn up a model statute that could be described as a 'comprehensive' model of regulation.

Trends in reforms of regulatory systems also support the 'comprehensive' and 'wide' models of regulation. In attempts to raise standards, the Australian states of Queensland and Victoria have reformed their regulatory systems from 'minimal' to more 'comprehensive' models. In the USA, Oregon and Washington have introduced regulation for the first time that is 'comprehensive', and several states (Florida, New York, Oklahoma, Tennessee, Utah and Virginia) have amended existing regulations to widen and or deepen regulation – again with the aim of raising standards. In Europe, Germany has recently moved from a 'minimal' to 'comprehensive' regulatory system and, in France and Spain, further widening and deepening are under consideration. In the Republic of Ireland a government discussion paper has recently been issued that proposes a 'comprehensive' and 'wide' system of regulation, which was subsequently introduced with the Private Security Services Bill 2001 (Government of Ireland 1997). In Hong Kong (just before it was handed back to the Chinese) the existing 'minimum narrow' system was re-formed into a 'comprehensive wide' system (Murphy 1996). Finally, in South Africa, a very extensive report into the system of regulation has recently recommended extending controls to the wider private security industry, including in-house security, private investigators, security consultants, door supervisors and polygraphists amongst many others. This system already had extensive controls for companies and minimum standards for training and experience (Security Officers Board 2000). If these reforms are implemented, this system will be one of the widest and deepest in the world. There is, therefore, evidence that supports the 'comprehensive' and 'wide' models of regulation described by George and Button (1997) as the model most jurisdictions are moving towards and as the best for raising standards in the industry. Nevertheless, this is still an area that requires further empirical research.

The Private Security Industry Act 2001

In 2001, after 30 years' campaigning for regulation in England and Wales and after the publication of numerous policy proposals, the Private Security Industry Act was finally passed (Younger 1972; Home Office 1979; HAC 1995; George and Button 1998). This legislation has established a new non-departmental public body (or QUANGO) called the Security Industry Authority (SIA). The SIA will have a board and chair chosen by the Home Secretary who will preside over a Chief Executive, his or her staff and an inspectorate. The SIA will have a wide range of functions but the most important will be the licensing of individuals operating in sectors of the private security industry that are subject to regulation. As the legislation stands this would encompass security officers in the contract static guarding and cash-in-transit sectors, door supervisors (contract and in-house), bodyguards, wheel-clampers (contract and in-house), private investigators and security consultants. Licences would be required for all employees, from the most junior to the most senior. The legislation also gives power to the Home Secretary to extend the coverage of the legislation to other sectors of the private security industry.

Licensing will be based upon an individual being a 'fit and proper' person. This includes a criminal records check through the Criminal Records Bureau and other conditions that could be imposed by the board through secondary legislation issued by the Home Secretary (e.g. minimum standards of training and adherence to a code of conduct). Door supervisors will be subject to a different form of licensing as the legislation allows existing local registration schemes to continue, but these could be reformed (or imposed if they don't already exist) by the Home Secretary through secondary legislation.

The legislation does not propose the *compulsory* licensing of firms but limits itself to a voluntary scheme firms may subject themselves to. The intention seems to be that the SIA will make use of some of the existing, voluntarily inspected regimes, such as those of the NSI. There would be scope, however, for the Home Secretary to issue a statutory instrument making these schemes compulsory.

The legislation has also created a new series of criminal offences. Managers of 'cowboy' firms who continue to use 'shady' practices could risk fines and imprisonment. For instance, a manager who knowingly employs unlicensed staff to act as security officers could be risking a lengthy prison sentence and a large fine. Similarly, security officers who apply for a licence knowingly using false information could also risk a fine and short prison sentence.

The legislation gives a great deal of discretion to the Home Secretary, Chief Executive, the chair and board of the SIA. For example, many of the finer details of the regime will be left to them to decide. Thus whoever is appointed to the board and chair will signal the likely future of the regulatory regime. Also, should a Home Secretary be appointed with a keen interest in deregulation (such as a future Conservative Home Secretary), new regulations could be blocked or watered down. He or she could even embark on a process of deregulation.

This Act is, in many ways, a dilution of the proposals set out in the white paper published in March 1999 (Home Office 1999). This is largely a result of the Better Regulation Initiative (the structures within government designed to reduce the burden of regulation on businesses). For instance, while alarm installers were one of the priorities for regulation in that paper, they were excluded from the legislation. The other significant sector that has disappeared is in-house manned guarding. However, on the positive side, private investigators, security consultants and wheel-clampers are in the primary legislation, while they were only a low priority in the white paper.

The exclusion of security systems installers represents a significant 'watering down' of the original proposals. The reason they were excluded is because there is no evidence of criminal actions ever having been taken against alarm installers. However, this leaves a number of issues unresolved: the significant drain on police resources because of false alarms from poorly installed alarms; the overall impact on crime rates security systems failures have; and the exposés of 'cowboy' installers. All these issues make the licensing of this sector a priority.

It is also essential that in-house staff are regulated as their exclusion could lead to unscrupulous operators exploiting this loophole. It could also lead to confusion. Imagine two shops next to one another, one with in-house (unlicensed) security staff and the other with contract (licensed) security staff. The former could quite legitimately employ individuals who are unable to secure a licence. Consider also a shopping centre owned by company X, but managed by a facilities management company Y that employs its own security staff. Would these be classed as in-house or contract? If the former, this would suggest a potential for exploitation by unscrupulous operators (Button and George 1998).

One of the main selling points of this legislation has been the crackdown on door supervisors. While local authority registration schemes have been a welcome development in the absence of national legislation, the proposed system of endorsing and amending existing schemes and of requiring other local authorities to introduce them will not be the most efficient means of tackling the problems associated with this sector. It will lead to two-tier licensing and varying levels of enforcement between the SIA and local authorities and *amongst* local authorities. Similarly, while local authorities should have a role to play in this because of their responsibility for licensing entertainment venues, the best way to tackle the problem of door supervisors is a national licence based upon common vetting and training standards. Local authorities could then enforce these provisions and administer local schemes.

The most serious weakness in the legislation is the 'approved contractors' scheme. What is proposed is little more than an elaborate version of the accreditation scheme that already exists through the United Kingdom Accreditation Service (UKAS). It is expected that some of the existing UKAS-approved inspectorates (such as the NSI) will be given these tasks. Under the current arrangements, large numbers of firms are not inspected by these inspectorates or by any other organisation. Many purchasers of security services will consider accreditation costs as a 'grudge cost', and they will hence purchase the cheapest. And there will always be firms who seek to gain a competitive advantage by cutting standards where they can. In the security market this will continue unless firms are forced to meet minimum standards. However, there is at least scope to turn this into a compulsory scheme but, ideally, this should have been made mandatory in the primary legislation.

While this legislation is to be welcomed as going some way towards achieving what the industry needs and deserves, if it is to meet the objective of raising standards, a number of statutory instruments must be issued to refine and extend the scope of the legislation to the wider private security industry and to establish tough, compulsory minimum standards that apply to firms as well as to employees. At the time of writing the first board members and Chief Executive were awaiting appointment. These appointments will be crucial to the development of an effective regulatory system.

Regulating policing: policing commissions revisited

The 'fragmentation' or 'pluralisation' of policing has led to some radical ideas about regulating the new policing order. While this chapter has focused largely on private security, private policing is a much broader issue and, clearly, debates about regulation and accountability also apply to this. Loader (2000) has criticised the existing models of control that are based upon specific sectors of policing and has sought to resurrect and redevelop the ideas of Jefferson and Grimshaw (1984) concerning police commissions. Loader (2000: 327) proposes the establishment of policing commissions at local, regional and national levels whose aim would be: 'to formulate policies and coordinate service delivery across the policing network, and to bring to democratic account the public, municipal, commercial and voluntary agencies that comprise it.'

The commissions would consist of elected and appointed members in order to ensure social representativeness. They would have three broad functions. First, they would be responsible for policy formulation and strategic co-ordination. This would encompass setting policies and targets for the state police and developing policing plans – largely at the local and regional levels. The second function relates to the authorising, licensing and subsidising of policing. This would involve operating a licensing system for private security firms and staff, as well as setting standards on human rights, anti-discriminatory and equal opportunities policies. The commission would issue tenders inviting voluntary, private and municipal bodies to provide policing services. Linked to this, they would seek to make good inequities in policing provision in specific areas by allocating state provision or by contracting in additional provision. The final function relates to monitoring, inspection and evaluation. These would include bringing different forms of policing to democratic account through the provision of information, through the inspection of policing agencies and through monitoring the extent to which the different agencies achieve their objectives.

These proposals are radical and require much further debate. There is, however, not the space to explore them in any depth here. Some questions, on the other hand, must be debated further. For instance, there may be a risk that giving the commissions the responsibility for a wider range of policing organisations (beyond the public police) might actually risk a greater centralisation of power. Questions also arise over what would happen to much of the existing infrastructure of police authorities, the HMIC, the PCA, etc. Would they be abolished or remain under the new system? Another issue that needs considering is the extent to which the policing commissions would apply to the extended policing community. Would they stretch to cover the responsibilities of such things as the RSPCA, benefit fraud investigators and health and safety inspectors, or would their scope be more restricted?

It could also be argued that a form of local policing commissions has already been created by the statutory partnerships mandated under the Crime and Disorder Act 1998. These bring together the police, local authority and other relevant local agencies to tackle crime and disorder and to develop a local strategy (Loveday 1999b). Membership of these partnerships varies, but there is clearly an overlap with the first set of functions identified for the commissions by Loader. Loveday (2000) has also argued that local authorities are better placed to tackle crime and disorder because of the much wider range of responsibilities they possess. These include planning, licensing, social services, education and the provision of leisure facilities, to name some of the most important. Thus Loader's proposals represent radical and innovative ideas to confront the growing plurality of policing, but they require much more debate and consideration.

Chapter 11

Private policing: concluding comments

The concept that the police represent only a part – albeit the most important part – of the policing infrastructure has become much more widely recognised in recent years. A wide range of public, private and 'hybrid' agents are engaged in the policing process. However, such are the changes that have taken place in society and in policing organisations that it has become much more difficult to identify the public, 'hybrid' and private sectors. Instead it has become more appropriate to consider policing bodies in terms of their degree of 'publicness' and 'privateness'. These changes have made the classification of policing much more complicated. Despite these challenges, however, it is possible to construct a classificatory model that provides a means for analysing and debating the complex web of policing.

The wide range of agents engaged in policing has led some to argue that a 'pluralisation' or 'fragmentation' of policing has taken place (Bayley and Shearing 1996; Johnston 2000a). There is little doubt that any analysis of policing in the UK would reveal a significant 'fragmentation' of policing. Indeed, this book has illustrated the large number of agents who are engaged in policing. However, to what extent this marks a new era in policing is more debatable. As Chapters 4–6 have illustrated, a large number of policing organisations have long histories, many having been established before the formation of the modern police. A fairer assessment would be that 'fragmentation' has been accelerating in recent years (particularly through the growth of private security and municipal policing); it does not represent a new trend. In seeking to identify theoretical explanations for these changes, the focus here has largely been upon private security. However, drawing conclusions from the broader range of organisations involved in policing poses new challenges for academics, and is an area in need of much more scholarly interest.

The emerging policing order also raises a number of issues policy-makers are only just beginning to grapple with. First there is the issue of the accountability and regulation, particularly in the private security industry. This book has explored the debate over the regulation of the private security industry and has analysed the structures that have been developed to bring greater regulation and accountability. In doing so it has identified some of the weaknesses of these structures. The increasing 'fragmentation' of policing, however, raises many concerns, and it is only now that academics are beginning to come to terms with this (Loader 2000). Perhaps the most important issue, however, is making some of the many 'hybrid' policing organisations more accountable. Many of these organisations have special powers and undertake important tasks that have a significant impact upon the public. Despite this there has been relatively little interest in this issue.

The second important issue concerns the co-operation between these different policing organisations, which goes beyond the oft-debated public–private relationship. There are in the 'hybrid' sector alone many organisations that would benefit from much greater co-operation, if not merger. Some already co-operate on issues with varying degrees of success and commitment. For instance, tackling fraud in the public sector is pursued by a multiplicity of organisations at both a central and de-centralised level. The resulting duplication and complexity undoubtedly lead to greater inefficiencies, yet there are no formal organisational structures to bring these bodies together. Indeed, there is a strong case for a national, public sector fraud police.

The government has begun to tackle this problem through its promotion of 'joined-up government'. This seeks to integrate the criminal justice system and it encourages and improves partnerships between agencies and local communities (Home Office 2001). However, beyond closer working relationships between the public police and the private sector, there is little to encourage the 'joining up' of policing. If a more efficient and effective criminal justice system is to be achieved, there must be commitment from all parties to a 'joined-up' policing agenda.

These concerns illustrate another significant issue: the need for more research into the individuals and organisations engaged in policing. Criminologists frequently debate the 'dark figure' in terms of the level and distribution of crime. There is also clearly a 'dark figure' when research into all those involved in policing is considered. This need for more research into private security has been identified already (Johnston 1992a; Reiner 2000a) and, despite a growing interest, this continues to be the case. Some of the many other organisations involved with policing should also be prioritised for further research. For example, there has been very little research into the many public organisations involved in investigating and countering fraud, such as the DWP (Department for Work and Pensions) and the NHS. The important role of trading standards officers has also been neglected. Given the growing concern with the environment and with animal welfare issues, it is surprising the RSPCA has received little attention. In the end there is a very wide range of organisations that deserve much greater attention from researchers.

It seems certain that, as the twenty-first century progresses, private policing as an issue will continue to grow in importance. There are already a number of British initiatives that will expand the role, improve the accountability and raise the profile of private security alone. Other areas of the policing infrastructure might also experience a similar growth in attention. At an international level, private policing is also likely to receive greater interest as the process of globalisation continues. The Belgian government had plans to raise the issue of private security regulation during its presidency of the EU in 2001. Other international forums could also become more preoccupied with private security and policing. Some of these might include the aviation industry (particularly in the light of the terrorist attacks on New York and Washington, DC), the maritime industry and Internet providers. These present further challenges to researchers and policy-makers. It is hoped this book has contributed to a greater understanding of private policing while also stimulating further interest and research in this burgeoning area.

References

Abrahams, R. (1998) *Vigilant Citizens.* Cambridge: Polity Press.

Atkinson, R. (1990) Government during the Thatcher years. In Savage, S., *et al* (eds.) *Public Policy in Britain.* Chatham: Mackays.

Audit Commission (1996) *Streetwise—Effective Police Patrol.* London: HMSO.

Bailey, S. (1992) *Cross on Principles of Local Government Law.* London: Sweet and Maxwell.

Baldry, E. (1996) Prison privateers: neo-colonialists in NSW. *Howard Journal* 35: 161–74.

Bayley, D. and Shearing, C.D. (1996) The future of policing. *Law and Society Review* 30: 585–606.

Baxter, J. (1990) *State Security, Privacy and Information.* London: Harvester Wheatsheaf.

Beck, A. and Willis, A. (1995) *Crime and Security: Managing the Risk to Safe Shopping.* Leicester: Perpetuity Press.

Beck, U. (1992) *Risk Society: Towards a New Modernity.* London: Sage.

Benn, S.I. and Gaus, G.F. (1983) The public and private: concepts and action. In Benn, S.I. and Gaus, G.F. (eds.) *Public and Private in Social Life.* London: Croom Helm.

Bennett, T.H. (1990) *Evaluating Neighbourhood Watch.* Aldershot: Gower.

Bennetto, J. (2001) Met to employ civilians on street patrol. *The Independent* 29 October.

Bergland, T. (u.d.) The security industry in Europe – how to act and react towards Europe. Unpublished Paper presented to the Confederation of European Security Services.

Birch, G. (1993) The security sham. *Police Review* 19 February.

Blair, I. (1998) Where do the police fit into policing? Speech delivered to ACPO Conference, 16 July.

Braun, M.A. and Lee, D.J. (1971) Private police forces: legal powers and limitations. *University of Chicago Law Review* 38: 555–82.

British Entertainment and Discotheque Association (BEDA) (1995) Memorandum of evidence. In Home Affairs Committee. *The Private Security Industry* Vol. 2, HC 17-II. London: HMSO.

British Retail Consortium (1999) *Retail Crime Survey 1998*. London: British Retail Consortium.

British Transport Police (2000) *Annual Report 1999–2000*. London: BTP.

Brown, R.M. (1975) *Strain of Violence*. New York: Oxford University Press.

Bryett, K. (1996) Privatisation – variation on a theme *Policing and Society* 6: 23–35.

Buncombe, A., Waugh, P. and Reeves, P. (1998) Firm was 'close' to £2m ransom deal. *The Independent* 10 December.

Bunyan, T. (1976) *The Political Police in Britain*. London: Julian Friedmann Publishers.

Burke, J. and Byrne, C. (1996) Revealed: How to hire your own policeman for £35 an hour. *The Sunday Times* 27 October.

Burrell, I. (1998) Police plan UK-wide roadblocks. *The Independent on Sunday* 12 August.

Burrows, W.E. (1976) *Vigilantes*. New York: Harcourt Brace Jovanovich.

Butler, S. (1991) Privatisation for public purposes. In W.T. Gormley (ed.) *Privatisation and its Alternatives*. Madison: University of Wisconsin Press.

Butler, T. (2000) Managing the future: a chief constable's view. In F. Leishman *et al* (eds.) *Core Issues in Policing* (2nd edn). London: Longman.

Button, M. (1998) 'Beyond the public gaze', the exclusion of private investigators from the British debate over regulating private security. *International Journal of the Sociology of Law* 26: 1–16.

Button, M. (1999) Private security and its contribution to policing: under-researched, under-utilised and underestimated. *International Journal of Police Science and Management* 2: 103–16.

Button, M. and George, B. (1994) Why some organisations prefer in-house to contract security staff. In M. Gill (ed.) *Studies in Security and Crime Prevention*. Leicester: Perpetuity Press.

Button, M. and George, B. (1998) Why some organisations prefer contract to in-house security staff. In M. Gill (ed.) *Crime at Work: Increasing the Risk for Offenders*. Leicester: Perpetuity Press.

Button, M. and George, B. (2001) Government regulation in the United Kingdom private security industry: the myth of non-regulation. *Security Journal* 14: 55–66.

Button, M. and John, T. (forthcoming) 'Plural policing' in action: a review of the policing of environmental protests in England and Wales. *Policing and Society*.

Button, M., John, T. and Brearley, N. (2001) *New Challenges in Public Order Policing – The Professionalisation of Environmental Protest and the Emergence of the Militant Environmental Activist*. Occasional Paper 14. Portsmouth: Institute of Criminal Justice Studies.

Cahalane, M. (2001) Reducing false alarms has a price – so does response: is the price worth paying? *Security Journal* 14: 31–54.

Cambell, G. and Reingold, B. (1994) Private security and public policing in Canada. *Juristat Service Bulletin*. Ottawa: Canadian Centre for Justice Statistics.

Carriere, K.D. and Erikson, R.V. (1989) *Crimestoppers: A Study in the Organisation of Community Policing*. Toronto: University of Toronto, Centre for Criminology.

Chaiken, M. and Chaiken, J. (1987) *Public Policing – Privately Provided*. Washington, DC: National Institute of Justice.

Chittenden, M. (2000) For hire: Britain's Keystone Cops. *The Sunday Times* 22 October.

Chu, Y.K. (1996) Triad societies and the business community in Hong Kong. *International Journal of Risk, Security and Crime Prevention* 1: 33–40.

Clayton, T. (1967) *The Protectors*. London: Oldbourne.

Cohen, S. (1985) *Visions of Social Control*. Cambridge: Polity.

Cohen, S. and Scull, A. (eds.) (1983) *Social Control and the State*. Oxford: Martin Robertson.

Collcutt, D. (1998) Viagra pills are seized at Soho bookshop. *The Times* 11 August.

Cook, R. (1999) *Dangerous Ground: The Inside Story of Britain's Leading Investigative Journalist*. London: HarperCollins.

Cooper, C. (1997) Shameful record of Jockey Club's Inspector Clouseau. *News of the World* 19 January.

Cornwall, H. (1991) *The Industrial Espionage Handbook*. London: Century.

Couch, S.R. (1987) Selling and reclaiming state sovereignty: the case of coal and iron police. *The Insurgent Sociologist* 4: 85–91.

Crimestoppers Trust (1997) *Annual Review 1996*. London: Crimestoppers Trust.

Cunningham, W.C., Strauchs, J.J. and Van Meter, C.W. (1990) *Private Security Trends 1970–2000. Hallcrest Report* II. Stoneham (USA): Butterworth-Heinemann.

Cunningham, W.C. and Taylor, T. (1985) *Private Security and Police in America*. (the Hallcrest report). Portland: Chancellor Press.

Dance, O.R. (1990) To what extent could or should policing be privatized? *Australian Police Journal* 45: 9–13.

Davies, S. (1996) *Big Brother – Britain's Web of Surveillance and the New Technological Order*. London: Macmillan.

Davis, M. (1990) *City of Quartz*. London: Vintage.

De Bruxelles, S. (2000) Fake aristocrat found guilty of benefit fraud. *The Times* 13 April.

Defence Committee (1996a) *Ministry of Defence Police and Guarding*. HC 189. London: HMSO.

Defence Committee (1996b) *Ministry of Defence Police and Guarding. Government Reply*. London: HMSO.

Department of Transport (1990) *Ports Police Forces – Consultation Paper*. Unpublished paper.

De Waard, J. (1993) The private security sector in fifteen European countries: size, rules and legislation. *Security Journal* 4: 58-62.

De Waard, J. (1999) The private security industry in international perspective. *European Journal of Criminal Policy and Research* 7: 143–74.

Donahue, J.D. (1989) *The Privatisation Decision*. New York: Basic Books.

Dover Harbour Board Police (1994) *Annual Report*. Dover: Dover Harbour Board Police.

Draper, H. (1978) *Private Police*. Sussex: Harvester Press.

Environment Agency (2000) *Annual Report and Accounts 1999–2000*. London: HMSO.

Environment Agency (2001) Website. Available: http://www.environment-agency.gov.uk (accessed: 19 June 2001).

Esler, G. (1983) The nuclear police: a secret police force with disquieting powers. *The Listener* 24 November: 5–6.

Federation Against Software Theft (FAST) (2001) Website. Available: http://www.fast.org.uk (accessed: 14 June 2001).

Feldman, D. (1986) *The Law Relating to Entry, Search and Seizure*. London: Butterworths.

Financial Services Authority (2001) What We Do (online). Available: http://www.fsa.gov.uk/what (accessed: 19 June 2001).

Flynn, N. (1997) *Public Sector Management*. Hemel Hempstead: Prentice-Hall.

Focault, M. (1977) *Discipline and Punish*. London: Allen Lane.

Forst, B. and Manning, P.K. (1999) *The Privatisation of Policing*. Washington, DC: George Washington University Press.

Francis, J. (1993) *The Politics of Regulation*. Oxford: Blackwell.

Frosdick, S. and Sidney, J. (1997) The evolution of safety management and stewarding at football grounds. In Frosdick, S. and Walley, L. (eds.) *Sport and Safety Management*. Oxford: Butterworth-Heinemann.

Gans, J. (2000) Privately paid public policing: law and practice. *Policing and Society* 10: 183–206.

Garland, D. (1996) The limits of sovereign state: strategies of crime control in contemporary Society. *British Journal of Criminology* 35: 445–71.

George, B. and Button, M. (1996) The case for regulation. *International Journal of Risk, Security and Crime Prevention* 1: 53–7.

George, B. and Button, M. (1997) Private security industry regulation: lessons from abroad for the United Kingdom. *International Journal of Risk, Security and Crime Prevention* 2: 187–200.

George, B. and Button, M. (1998) 'Too little too late': a critique of recent policy proposals for the private security industry in the United Kingdom. *Security Journal* 10: 1–7.

George, B. and Button, M. (2000) *Private Security*. Leicester: Perpetuity Press.

Giddens, A. (1990) *The Consequences of Modernity*. Cambridge: Polity Press.

Gill, M. (1987) The Special Constabulary: community representation and accountability. In Mawby, R.I. (ed.) *Policing Britain*. Plymouth: Plymouth Polytechnic.

Gill, M. (ed.) (1994) *Crime at Work: Studies in Security and Crime Prevention*. Leicester: Perpetuity Press.

Gill, M. (ed.) (1998) *Crime at Work: Increasing the Risk for Offenders. Volume II*. Leicester: Perpetuity Press.

Gill, M. and Hart, J. (1997a) Exploring investigative policing. *British Journal of Criminology* 37: 549–67.

Gill, M. and Hart, J. (1997b) Policing as a business: the organisation and structure of private investigation. *Policing and Society* 7: 117–41.

Gill, M., Hart, J. and Stevens, J. (1996) Private investigators: under-researched, under-estimated, under-used? *International Journal of Risk, Security and Crime Prevention* 1: 305–16.

Gilling, D. (1997) *Crime Prevention – Theory, Policy and Politics*. London: UCL Press.

Gladwin, I. (1974) *The Sheriff: The Man and his Office*. London: Victor Gollancz.

Goodwin, M. (1996) Local authority – lawful authority? An examination of Wandsworth Parks Police arrests and the interaction with the Metropolitan Police on the Battersea Division. Unpublished dissertation for the BSc in Policing and Police Studies, University of Portsmouth.

Government of Ireland (1997) *Report of the Consultative Group on the Private Security Industry*. Dublin: Stationary Office.

Gregory, M. (1994) *Dirty Tricks – British Airways' Secret War against Virgin Atlantic*. London: Little Brown & Co.

Group 4 Falck (2001) Group 4 Falck in brief (online). Available: http://www.group4securitas.com/object.php?obj=obj34000c (accessed: 14 September 2001).

Harding, R.W. (1997) *Private Prisons and Public Accountability*. Buckingham: Open University Press.

Hayek, F.A. (1960) *The Constitution of Liberty*. London: Routledge & Keegan Paul.

Health and Safety Commission (1996) *Annual Report 1995–96*. London: HSE Books.

Health and Safety Executive (2001) Website. Available: http://www.hse.gov.uk/press/e99030 (accessed: 16 March 2001).

Hencke, D. (1998) Easy living for fraud investigators. *The Guardian*, 13 August.

Herbert, S. (1999) The end of the territorial-sovereign state? The case of crime control in the United States. *Political Geography* 18: 149–72.

HM Customs and Excise (1997) *Annual Report 1996–97*. Cm 3776. London: HMSO.

HM Customs and Excise (2001) HM Customs and Excise (online). Available: http://www.hmce.gov.uk/general/about/dep-over.htm (accessed: 23 February 2001).

Hobbs, D., Hall, S., Winlow, S., Lister, S. and Hadfield, P. (2000) *Bouncers: The Art and Economics of Intimidation*. ESRC Violence Research Programme, final report. Swindon: ESRC.

Hobbs, D., Lister, S., Hadfield, P., Winlow, S. and Hall, S. (2000) Receiving shadows: governance and liminality in the night-time economy. *British Journal of Sociology* 51: 701–17.

Hobsbawn, E.J. (1959) *Primitive Rebels*. Manchester: Manchester University Press.

Home Affairs Committee (HAC) (1995) *The Private Security Industry. Volumes I and II*. HC 17 I and II. London: HMSO.

Home Office (1979) *The Private Security Industry: A Discussion Paper*. London: HMSO.

Home Office (1995) *Review of Police Core and Ancillary Tasks: Final Report*. London: HMSO.

Home Office (1999) *The Government's Proposals for the Regulation of the Private Security Industry in England and Wales*. Cm 4254. London: HMSO.

Home Office (2001) *Criminal Justice: The Way Ahead*. Cm 5074. London: HMSO.

Hopkins-Burke, R. (ed.) (1998) *Zero Tolerance Policing*. Leicester: Perpetuity Press.

Hutter, B. (1988) *The Reasonable Arm of the Law: The Law Enforcement Procedures of Environmental Health Officers*. Oxford: Clarendon Press.

I'Anson, J. and Wiles, P. (undated) *The Sedgefield Community Force*. Sheffield: Centre for Criminological and Legal Research, University of Sheffield.

Immigration and Nationality Directorate (IND) (1999) Annual report 1999 (online). Available: http://www.homeoffice.gov.uk/ind/latest_info latest_info_contents01.htm (accessed:25 January 2001).

Inland Revenue (1999) *Annual Report for year ending March 1999*. London: Inland Revenue.

International Chamber of Commerce (ICC) (2001) Introducing the International Chamber of Commerce (online). Available: http://www.iccwbo.org/home/intro_icc/introducing_icc.asp (accessed: 14 June 2001).

International Chamber of Commerce Commercial Crime Bureau (ICCCCB) (2001) Website (online). Available: http://www.iccwbo.org/ccs/menu_ccb_bureau.asp (accessed 14 June 2001).

International Chamber of Commerce Commercial Crime Services (ICCCCS) (2001) Website (online). Available: http://www.iccwbo.org/index_ccs.asp (accessed: 14 June, 2001).

International Chamber of Commerce Counterfeiting Intelligence Bureau (ICCCIB) (2001) Website (online]. Available: http://www.iccwbo.org/ccs/menu_cib_bureau.asp (accessed: 14 June, 2001).

International Chamber of Commerce Cybercrime Unit (ICCCU) (2001) Website (online). Available: http://www.iccwbo.org/ccs/menu_cybercrime_unit.asp [accessed: 14 June 2001].

International Chamber of Commerce International Maritime Bureau (IMB) (2001) Website (online). Available: http://www.iccwbo.org/ccs/menu_imb_bureau.asp (accessed: 14 June 2001).

Jacobsen, J. and Saville, E. (1999) *Neighbourhood Warden Schemes: An Overview*. *CRRS Paper* 2. London: Home Office.

James, A.J., Bottomley, A.K., Liebling, A. and Clare, E. (1997) *Privatizing Prisons: Rhetoric or Reality.* London: Sage.

Jefferson, T. and Grimshaw, R. (1984) *Controlling the Constable: Police Accountability in England and Wales.* London: Cobden Trust.

Jenkins, C. (1998) Civil defence. *Police Review* 20 February.

Jessop, B. (1993) Towards a Schumpeterian workfare state? Preliminary remarks on post-Fordism: alternative perspectives on economic and political change. *Economy and Society* 24: 7–39.

Johnston, L. (1991) Privatisation and the police function: from 'new police' to 'new policing'. In Reiner, R. and Cross, M. (eds.) *Beyond Law and Order: Criminal Justice Policy and Politics in the 1990s.* Basingstoke: Macmillan.

Johnston, L (1992a) *The Rebirth of Private Policing.* London: Routledge.

Johnston, L. (1992b) An unseen force: the Ministry of Defence Police in the UK. *Policing and Society* 3: 23–40.

Johnston, L. (1994) Policing plutonium: issues in the provision of policing services at nuclear facilities and for related materials in transit. *Policing and Society* 4: 53–72.

Johnston, L. (1996) What is vigilantism? *British Journal of Criminology* 36: 220–36.

Johnston, L. (2000a) *Policing Britain: Risk, Security and Governance.* London: Longman.

Johnston, L. (2000b) Transnational private policing: the impact of global commercial security. In J.W.E. Sheptycki (ed.) *Issues in Transnational Policing.* London: Routledge.

Jones, T. and Newburn, T. (1995) How big is the private security industry? *Policing and Society* 5: 221–32.

Jones, T. and Newburn, T. (1998) *Private Security and Public Policing.* Oxford: Clarendon Press.

Judd, T. (2000) Tony Martin, the harmless eccentric whose obsession made him a killer. *The Independent.* 20 April.

Kakalik, J. and Wildhorn, S. (1971a) *Private Police in the United States: Findings and Recommendations. Vol. 1.* Washington, DC: Government Printing Office.

Kakalik, J. and Wildhorn, S. (1971b) *The Private Police Industry: Its Nature and Extent. Vol. 2.* Washington, DC: Government Printing Office.

Kakalik, J. and Wildhorn, S. (1971c) *Current Regulation of Private Police: Regulatory Agency Experience and Views. Vol. 3.* Washington, DC: Government Printing Office.

Kakalik, J. and Wildhorn, S. (1971d) *The Law and Private Police. Vol. 4.* Washington, DC: Government Printing Office.

Kakalik, J. and Wildhorn, S. (1971e) *Special Purpose Public Police. Vol. 5.* Washington, DC: Government Printing Office.

Kelling, G., Pate, T., Diekman, D. and Brown, C. (1974) *The Kansas City Preventative Experiment.* Washington, DC: Police Foundation.

Klandermans, B. (1997) *The Social Psychology of Protest.* Oxford: Blackwell.

Kowalewski, D. (1982) Establishment vigilantism and political dissent: a Soviet case study. *Armed Forces and Society* 9: 83–97.

Kowalewski, D. (1996) Countermovement vigilantism and human rights. *Crime, Law and Social Change* 25: 63–81.

Laurance, J. (1999) NHS to appoint 600 fraudbusters. *The Independent* 15 March.

Leake, J. (1998) Police chief quits over threat to nuclear plants. *The Sunday Times* 26 April.

Leishman, F., Cope, S. and Starie, P. (1996) Reinventing and restructuring: towards a 'new policing order'. In Leishman, F. *et al* (eds.) *Core Issues in Policing*. London: Longman.

Leishman, F., Loveday, B. and Savage, S. (eds.) (2000) *Core Issues in Policing* (2nd edn). London: Longman.

Leppard, D. and Rufford, N. (1998) Arms to Africa: no prosecution. *The Sunday Times* 17 May.

Liberty (1995) Memorandum of Evidence. In House of Commons Home Affairs Committee, *The Private Security Industry. Vol. II*. London: HMSO.

Lidstone, K.W., Hogg, R. and Sutcliffe, F. (1980) *Prosecutions by Private Individuals and Non-Police Agencies. Royal Commission on Criminal Procedure, Research Study* 10. London: HMSO.

Lilley, J.R. and Knepper, P. (1992) An international perspective on the privatisation of corrections. *Howard Journal* 31: 174–91.

Lister, S., Hobbs, D., Hall, S. and Winlow, S. (2000) Violence in the night-time economy; bouncers: the reporting, recording and prosecution of assaults. *Policing and Society* 10: 383–402.

Livingstone, K and Hart, J. (forthcoming) *The Wrong Arm of the Law? Public Images of Private Security*.

Loader, I. (1997) Private security and the demand for protection in contemporary Britain. *Policing and Society* 7:143–62.

Loader, I. (2000) Plural policing and democratic governance. *Social and Legal Studies* 9: 323–45.

Local Authority Investigation Officers Group (LAIOG) (1997) Memorandum of evidence. In Social Security Committee, *Housing Benefit Fraud*. HC 90-II. Vol I. London: HMSO.

Loveday, B. (1993) *Civilian Staff in the Police Force. Research Paper* 2. Leicester: Centre for the Study of Public order.

Loveday, B. (1998) Improving the status of Police Patrol. *International Journal of the Sociology of the Law* 26: 161–96.

Loveday, B. (1999a) Managing the police. In S. Horton and D. Farnham (eds.) *Public Management in Britain*. Basingstoke: Macmillan.

Loveday, B. (1999b) Tough on crime or tough on the causes of crime? An evaluation of Labour's crime and disorder legislation. *Crime Prevention and Community Safety: An International Journal* 1: 7–24.

Loveday, B. (2000) New directions in accountability In Leishman *et al* (eds.) (2000) *Core Issues in Policing* (2nd edn). London: Longman.

Macauley, S. (1986) Private government. In L. Lipson and S. Wheeler (eds.) *Law and the Social Sciences*. New York: Russell Sage Foundation.

MacErlean, N. (1997) Benefit spies join police road checks. *The Observer*, 2 February.

Mann, M. (1993) Nation states in Europe and other continents: diversifying, developing, not dying. *Daedalus* 122: 115–40.

Manunta, G. (1999) What is security? *Security Journal* 12: 57–66.

Marx, G. (1987) The interweaving of public and private police. In C.D. Shearing, and P.C. Stenning (eds.) *Private Policing*. Newbury Park, CA: Sage.

Mathews, R. (1989) Privatisation in perspective. In R. Mathews (ed.) *Privatising Criminal Justice*. London: Sage.

McCartney, J. (1996) Volunteer villagers get PCs back on the beat. *The Sunday Telegraph* 15th September.

McKenzie, I.K. and Gallagher, G.P. (1989) *Behind the Uniform: Policing in Britain and America*. Hemel Hempstead: Harvester Wheatsheaf.

McManners, H. (1997) Army may join battle on crime. *The Sunday Times*, 9 February.

McManus, M. (1995) *From Fate to Choice: Private Bobbies, Public Beats*. Aldershot: Avebury.

Medicines Control Agency (2000) *Annual Report 1999–2000*. London: HMSO.

Medicines Control Agency (2001) About the Agency (Online). Available: http://www.open.gov.uk/mca/mcahome.htm (accessed 19 June).

Miller, J.P. and Luke, D.E. (1977) *Law Enforcement by Public Officials and Special Police Forces*. London: Home Office.

Mills, H. (1998) From vice town to vigilante hell. *The Observer* 6 December.

Ministry of Defence Police (MDP) (2000) *Annual Report and Accounts 1999–2000*. HC 609. London: HMSO.

Moore, R.H. (1990) Licensing and Regulation of the private security industry: a historic view of the court's role. *Journal of Security Administration* 13: 37–61.

Morgan, R. and Newburn, T. (1997) *The Future of Policing*. Oxford: Oxford University Press.

Murphy, F. (1996) Control of the Security Industry in Hong Kong. Unpublished Dissertation, Scarman Centre for the Study of Public Order, University of Leicester.

Murray, G. (1993) *Enemies of the State*. London: Simon & Schuster.

National Advisory Committee on Criminal Standards and Goals (1976) *Private Security. Report of the Task Force on Private Security*. Washington, DC: Government Printing Office.

National Audit Office (1997) *Measures to Combat Housing Benefit Fraud*. HC 164. London: HMSO.

National Society for the Prevention of Cruelty to Children (NSPCC) (2000) *1999 Annual Report*. London: NSPCC.

National Society for the Prevention of Cruelty to Children (NSPCC) (2001) Homepage (Online). Available: http://www.nspcc.org.uk/homepage (Accessed 14 June).

Newburn, T. and Jones, T. (1997) *Policing After the Act*. London: PSI.

Noaks, L. (2000) Private cops on the block: a review of the role of private security in residential communities. *Policing and Society* 10: 143–61.

Norman, P. and Russell, P. (2000) *Nature of Public Sector Fraud and Corruption and Counter Fraud Strategies.* Distance Learning Course for Certificate of Higher Education in Counter Fraud and Criminal Justice Studies. Portsmouth: Institute of Criminal Justice Studies, University of Portsmouth.

Norris, C., Moran, J. and Armstrong, G. (eds.) (1998) *Surveillance, Closed Circuit Television and Social Control.* Aldershot: Ashgate.

Norton-Taylor, R. and Black, I. (1998) Spooks in the Dark. *The Guardian*, 5 May.

Nozick, R. (1974) *Anarchy, State and Utopia.* Oxford: Blackwell.

O'Leary, D. (1994) Reflections on police privatisation. *FBI Law Enforcement Bulletin* September: 21–5.

O'Malley, P. and Palmer, D. (1996) Post-Keynesian Policing. *Economy and Society* 25: 137–55.

Onslow, R. (1992) *Great Racing Gambles and Frauds.* Swindon: Marlborough Books.

Oppal, W.T. (1994) *Closing the Gap – Policing and the Community; Use of Non-Police Personnel Excerpts.* The report of policing in the British Columbia Commission Report of Inquiry.

Osborne, D. and Gaebler, T. (1992) *Reinventing Government: How the Entrepreneurial Spirit is Transforming the Public Sector.* Reading, MA: Addison-Wesley.

Ostrowe B., B. and DiBiase, R. (1983) Citizen involvement as a crime deterrent: a study of public attitudes towards an unsanctioned citizen patrol group. *Journal of Political Science and Administration* 11:185–93.

Pengelly, R. (2001) The case for regionalisation. *Police* January.

Perry, K. (2000) Vigilante mob forces family into hiding. *The Guardian* 8 August.

Police Complaints Authority (PCA) (1995) *Annual Report 1994–95.* London: HMSO.

Police Complaints Authority (PCA) (2000) Annual Report 1999-2000 (online). Available: http://www.pca.gov.uk/pdfs/repo2000.pdf (accessed: 3 March 2001).

Police Federation (1995) *Survey of Public Attitudes to Policing.* Surbiton: Police Federation.

Police Foundation and Policy Studies Institute Independent Inquiry (PF/PSI) (1996) *The Role and Responsibilities of the Police.* London: PF/PSI.

Policy Action Team 6 (2000) *Neighbourhood Wardens.* London: Home Office.

Povey, D., Prime, J. and Taylor, P. (1998) *Notifiable Offences England and Wales 1997. Home Office Statistical Bulletin.* London: Government Statistical Service.

Prenzler, T. and Sarre, R. (1999) A survey of security legislation and regulatory strategies in Australia. *Security Journal* 12: 7–17.

Prison Officers Association (1997) Memorandum of Evidence. In Home Affairs Committee, *The Management of the Prison Service (Public and Private).* HC57-II. London: HMSO.

Radiocommunications Agency (2001a) Enforcement (online). Available: http://www.radio.gov.uk/document/busrev/96_97/keepspe.htm (accessed: 16 February 2001).

Radiocommunications Agency (2001b) Prosecution statistics (online). Available: http://www.radio.gov.uk/document/annual/98_99/page7.htm (accessed: 19 June 2001).

Rawlings, P. (1995) The idea of policing: a history. *Policing and Society* 5: 129–49.

Reiner, R. (1992) Police research in the United Kingdom. In M. Tonry and N. Morris (eds.) *Modern Policing: Crime and Justice: A Review of Research.* Chicago, IL: University of Chicago Press.

Reiner, R. (1994) Policing and the police. In M. Maguire *et al* (eds.) *The Oxford Handbook of Criminology.* Oxford: Oxford University Press.

Reiner, R. (2000a) Police research. In R.D. King and E. Wincup (eds.) *Doing Research on Crime and Justice.* Oxford: Oxford University Press.

Reiner, R. (2000b) *The Politics of the Police.* Oxford: Oxford University Press.

Reiss, A.J. (1988) *Private Employment of Public Police.* Washington, DC: National Institute of Justice.

Reynolds, C. and Wilson, P. (1997) Private policing: creating new options. In D. Chappell and P. Wilson (eds.) *Australian Policing: Contemporary Policing.* Sydney: Butterworths.

Rhodes, R.A.W. (1995) *The New Governance: Governing without Government.* ESRC State of Britain Seminar II. Swindon: ESRC.

Rose, N. (1996) The death of the social? Refiguring the territory of government. *Economy and Society* 25: 359–97.

Rosenbaum, H.J. and Sedeberg, P.C. (eds.) (1976) *Vigilante Politics.* Philadelphia, PA: University of Pennsylvania Press.

Rothbard, M.N. (1978) *For a New Liberty: The Libertarian Manifesto.* New York: Collier Macmillan.

Rowlingson, K., Whyley, C., Newburn, T. and Berthoud, R. (1997) *Social Security Fraud: The Role of Penalties. Research Report* 64. London: HMSO.

Royal Air Force Police (1993) *75 Years of the Royal Air Force Police.* Fairford: RAF Benevolent Fund Enterprises.

Royal Society for the Prevention of Cruelty to Animals (RSPCA) (2000) *Trustees' Report and Accounts 1999.* Horsham: RSPCA.

Royal Society for the Prevention of Cruelty to Animals (2001) RSPCA facts (online). Available: http://www.rspca.org.uk/content/about_rspca/rspca.html (accessed: 14 June 2001).

Royal Society for the Protection of Birds (RSPB) Investigations Section (1999) *Birdcrime 98: Offences against the Wild Bird Legislation in 1998.*

Sarre, R. (1994) The legal powers of private police and security providers. In P. Moyle (ed.) *Private Prisons and Police – Recent Australian Trends.* Leichhardt, NSW: Pluto Press.

Sarre, R. and Prenzler, T. (1999) The regulation of private policing: reviewing mechanisms of accountability. *Crime Prevention and Community Safety: An International Journal* 1: 17–28.

Savage, S., Charman, S. and Cope, S. (2001) *Policing and the Power of Persuasion*. London: Blackstone Press.

Scott, T.M. and MacPherson, M. (1971) The development of the private sector of the criminal justice system. *University of Chicago Law Review* 6: 267–88.

Scottish Society for the Prevention of Cruelty to Animals (2001) Inspectorate (online). Available: http://www.scottishspca.org (accessed: 14 June 2001).

Security Officers Board (2000) *Principles Regarding the Future Regulation of the Occupation of Security Officers and Related Matters – Policy Paper*. Pretoria, South Africa: Security Officers Board.

Serious Fraud Office (SFO) (1997) *Annual Report 1996–97*. London: SFO.

Sharp, D. and Wilson, D. (2000) 'Household security': private policing and vigilantism in Doncaster. *Howard Journal* 39:113–31.

Shearer, D. (1998) *Private Armies and Military Intervention. Adelphi Paper* 316. Oxford: Oxford University Press.

Shearing, C.D. (1992) The relation between public and private policing. In M. Tonry and N. Morris (eds.) *Modern Policing. Vol. 15*. Chicago, IL: University of Chicago Press.

Shearing, C.D. (1993) Policing: relationships between public and private forms. In M. Findlay and U. Zvekic (eds.) *Alternative Policing Styles*. Boston, MA: Kluwer Law and Taxation Publishers.

Shearing, C.D. (1996) Public and private policing. In W. Saulsbury *et al* (eds.) *Themes in Contemporary Policing*. London: Policy Studies Institute.

Shearing, C.D. and Stenning, P.C. (1981) Modern private security: its growth and implications. In M. Tonry and N. Morris (eds.) *Crime and Justice: An Annual Review of Research*. Chicago, IL: University of Chicago Press.

Shearing, C.D. and Stenning, P.C. (1982) *Private Security and Private Justice*. Montreal: The Institute on Public Policy.

Shearing, C.D. and Stenning, P.C. (eds) (1987a) *Private Policing*. Newbury Park, CA: Sage.

Shearing, C.D. and Stenning, P.C. (1987b) Say 'cheese!': the Disney order that is not so Mickey Mouse. In C.D. Shearing and P.C. Stenning (eds.) *Private Policing*. Newbury Park, CA: Sage.

Shearing, C.D., Stenning, P.C. and Addario, S.M. (1985) Police perceptions of private security. *Canadian Police College Journal* 9: 127–53.

Sheptycki, J.W.E. (1998) Policing, postmodernism and transnationalisation. *British Journal of Criminology* 38: 485–503.

Sherman, L. (1990) Police crackdown: initial and residual deterrence. In M. Tonry and N. Morris (eds.) *Crime and Justice A Review of Research. Vol. 12*. Chicago, IL: University of Chicago Press.

Shichor, D. (1995) *Punishment for Profit*. Thousand Oaks, CA: Sage.

Shotland, R.L. and Goodstein, L.I. (1984) The role of bystanders in crime control. *Journal of Social Issues* 40: 9–26.

Shotland, R.L. and Stebbins, C.A. (1980) Bystander response to rape. Can a victim attract help? *Journal of Applied Social Psychology* 10: 510–27.

Silke, A. (1998) The lords of discipline: the methods and motives of paramilitary vigilantism in Northern Ireland. *Low Intensity Conflict and Law Enforcement* 7: 121–56.

Silke, A. (1999) Ragged justice: loyalist vigilantism in Northern Ireland. *Terrorism and Political Violence* 11: 1–31.

Silke, A. and Taylor, M. (2000) War without end: comparing IRA and loyalist vigilantism in Northern Ireland. *Howard Journal* 39: 249–66.

Slater, T. (1982) Regulation, standards and goals for the private security industry. *Police Review* 26 February.

Smith, D. and Visher, C.A. (1981) Street level justice: situational determinants of police arrest decisions. *Social Problems* 29: 169–77.

Social Security Committee (1997) *Housing Benefit Fraud*. HC 90–II. Vol. I. London: HMSO.

South, N. (1988) *Policing for Profit*. London: Sage.

Spencer, P. (1994) You've been framed. *Manchester Evening News*, 24 September.

Spitzer, S. (1987) Security and control in capitalist societies: the fetishism of security and the secret thereof. In J. Lowman *et al* (eds.) *Transcarceration: Essays in the Sociology of Social Control*. Aldershot: Gower.

Spitzer, S. and Scull, A.T. (1977) Privatisation and the capitalist development of the police. *Social Problems* 25:18–29.

Stenning, P.C. (1989) Private police and public police: toward a redefinition of the police role. In D.J. Loree (ed.) *Future Issues in Policing: Symposium Proceedings*. Ottawa: Canadian Police College.

Stenning, P.C. (1994) Private policing – some recent myths, developments and trends. In D. Biles and J. Vernon (eds.) *Private Sector and Community Involvement in the Criminal Justice System. Proceedings of a Conference held 30th November to 2nd December 1992 in Wellington, New Zealand*. Canberra: Australian Institute of Criminology.

Stenning, P.C. and Shearing, C.D. (1979a) *Search and Seizure: Powers of Private Security Personnel. A Study Paper Prepared for the Law Reform Commission of Canada*. Ottawa: Law Reform Commission of Canada.

Stenning, P. and Shearing, C.D. (1979b) Private security and private justice. *British Journal of Law and Society* 6: 261–71.

Stenning, P.C. and Shearing, C.D. (1980) The quiet revolution: the nature, development and general legal implications of private security in Canada. *Criminal Law Quarterly* 22: 220–48.

Stokes, P. (2000) Condemned meat fraudsters jailed. *Daily Telegraph*, 23 December.

Strange, S. (1996) *The Retreat of the State: The Diffusion of Power in the World Economy*. Cambridge: Cambridge University Press.

Syal, R. (2001) Rent-a-cop scheme to beat car thieves. *Sunday Telegraph*, 11 March.

Thames Valley Police (2001) Website (online). Available: http://www.thamesvalley.police.uk/income/income.htm (accessed: 22 February 2001).

TV Licensing (2001) Website (online). Available: http://www.tvlicensing.co.uk (accessed: 23 March 2001).

United Kingdom Atomic Energy Authority (2000) Chief Constable's annual report 1999–2000 (online). Available: http://www.ukae.org.uk/about/constab2k/APPENDIX%20Bhtm (accessed: 3 March).

United Kingdom Atomic Energy Authority Constabulary (UKAEAC) (1999) Chief Constable's annual report 1998–99 (online). Available: http://wwwukaea.org.uk/about/c-report/person.htm (accessed: 3 March 2001).

United States Committee on Education and Labor (1971) *Private Police Systems.* New York: Arno Press and the New York Times.

Vaughan, S. (2000) Man's best friend left tattered and torn – all done in the name of sport. *The News*, 2 August.

Vehicle Inspectorate (1993) *Annual Report 1992–93.* Bristol: Vehicle Inspectorate.

Vidal, J. (1996a) Bailiffs 'were reckless' in bypass clash. *The Guardian* 5 March.

Vidal, J. (1996b) My time as a Newbury security guard. *The Guardian* 25 January.

Vidal, J. (1997) *McLibel – Burger Culture on Trial.* London: Macmillan.

Waddington, P.A.J. (1999) *Policing Citizens.* London: UCL Press.

Walker, A. (1999) *The Safer Doors Project.* London: Home Office.

Walker, N. (2000) Transnational contexts. In F. Leishman *et al* (eds.) *Core Issues in Policing* (2nd edn). London: Longman.

Wall, D. (1998) *The Chief Constables of England and Wales.* Aldershot: Ashgate.

Waters, I. (2000) Quality and performance monitoring. In F. Leishman *et al* (eds.) *Core Issues in Policing* (2nd edn). London: Longman.

Weber, M. (1948) Politics as a vocation. In H.H. Gerth and C.W. Mills (eds. and translators) *From Max Weber: Essays in Sociology.* London: Routledge & Kegan Paul.

Weiss, R. (1978) The emergence and transformation of private detective and industrial policing in the United States, 1850–1940. *Crime and Social Justice* 1: 35–48.

Wiles, P. and McClintock, F. (eds.) (1972) *The Security Industry in the United Kingdom.* Cambridge: Institute of Criminology, University of Cambridge.

Wheelwright, J. (1998) Guardian Angels: the new buddies of surburbia. *The Independent* 13 July.

Wood, G. (2000) Jockeys' leader hits out at security purge. *The Independent* 8 December.

Yoshida, N. (1999) The taming of the Japanese private security industry. *Policing and Society* 9: 241–61.

Younger, K. (1972) *Report on the Committee on Privacy.* Cm 5012. London: HMSO.

Index